The Nitty Gritty

of
Teaching Adult Sunday School©

Step-by-Step

Curtis C. Mosley

Copyright 2007

The Sample Lessons in the back of the book may be copied.

Inquiries may be directed to:

Curtis Mosley
P.O. Box 1017
New Caney, TX. 77357

(281) 359-5577
CCMosley@earthlink.net

Dedication
To Christian Life Center
Birthplace of Ministries.

"Did not our heart burn within us, while he talked with us by the way, and while he opened to us the scriptures?" (Luke 24:32)

With special thanks to three great professors at Trinity Theological Seminary:

- Dr. Katheryn Webb

    "What makes a teacher a teacher" is being sensitive to the class during the lesson, and adjusting based on the Holy Spirit's leading.

- Dr. Max Sturdivant

    "At the end of the day, the life we lead is the real Bible lesson."

- Dr. E. E. Elliot

    - *"No word of God is without power."*

    - **The meaning of God's name "I AM" is "The One Who is always present." (Exodus 3:14)**

With thanks to editors Mike Chaffin, J. R. Hollingsworth.

Special recognition to Pam Schmidt of PS Graphics, Inc.

Contents

Introduction 7

Chapter 1	A Teacher is a Minister, Salesman, and Visionary Leader	9
Chapter 2	The Benefits of Being a Teacher	11
Chapter 3	Don't Teach Without These 10 Things	13
Chapter 4	The Personal Life of the Teacher	17
Chapter 5	Why They Come to Class and How This Can Help You	19
Chapter 6	Seeing the Person Your Student Will Become	21
Chapter 7	First Things First: Spiritual Warfare	23
Chapter 8	Paul's Pattern for Presentations	27
Chapter 9	Preparing and Delivering the Lesson	30
Chapter 10	Butterflies, Nerves, and Palpitations	41
Chapter 11	Useful In-Class Comments	43
Chapter 12	Preparation Checklist	45
Chapter 13	The Best Thing a Student Can Give a Teacher: A Question	47
Chapter 14	The Best Thing a Teacher Can Give a Student: A Compliment	49
Chapter 15	A Word About Attendance	51
Chapter 16	Why Stories Work	53
Chapter 17	Jesus' Favorite Teaching Technique	55
Chapter 18	A Picture is Worth a Thousand Words	57
Chapter 19	30 Ways to Mess Up Your Class	59
Chapter 20	Know Your Own Teaching Style	63

Sample Lessons

Chapter 21	Sample Lesson: God's Will	65
Chapter 22	Sample Lesson: Freedom from Sin	75
Chapter 23	Sample Lesson: Spiritual Warfare	81
Chapter 24	Sample Lesson: Prayer	91
Chapter 25	Sample Lesson: Teamwork	101
Chapter 26	Sample Lesson: Suffering	109
Chapter 27	Sample Lesson: Joy	117
Chapter 28	Sample Lesson: God's Sovereignty	121
Chapter 29	Sample Lesson: Divine Healing	126
Chapter 30	Sample Lesson: Heaven	133
Chapter 31	Sample Lesson: Money Management	141
Chapter 32	Sample Lesson: Taking the Name of God in Vain	151
Chapter 33	Sample Lesson: Interpersonal Communication	156
INDEX		164

Introduction

Oftentimes, we are called upon to teach the Bible, whether in Sunday School or home Bible studies. However, we are not often told HOW to teach, which seems unfair and stressful. If you are going to be given responsibility, shouldn't you be given appropriate instruction?

By learning the techniques in this book, you will be able to confidently approach your teaching assignment, knowing that you are fully capable of:

1. **Handling the spiritual demands of leading a Christian group.**

2. **Constructing a scripturally sound lesson.**

3. **Teaching in an appealing, organized and enjoyable manner.**

4. **Helping your students become more like Christ.**

This book shows you how to create a sound lesson on a Bible topic in only four steps:

1. SEED
The biblical definition of the topic.

2. NEED
The benefits of knowing this information and the consequences of ignorance.

3. FEED
The scriptures and information pertaining to the topic.

4. DEED
How to apply the lesson in specific steps.

You will also learn about the spiritual qualifications of the teacher, protecting your integrity, and the honors of being a teacher. Furthermore, the book provides a number of checklists to prepare you for teaching the lesson. Finally, there are sample lessons that illustrate how your finished product should look. (The six sample lessons are *not* copyright protected).

You will enjoy this straightforward, powerful method for writing and teaching topical Bible lessons. You will also gain a deeper appreciation for your ministry and your significance in God's Kingdom.

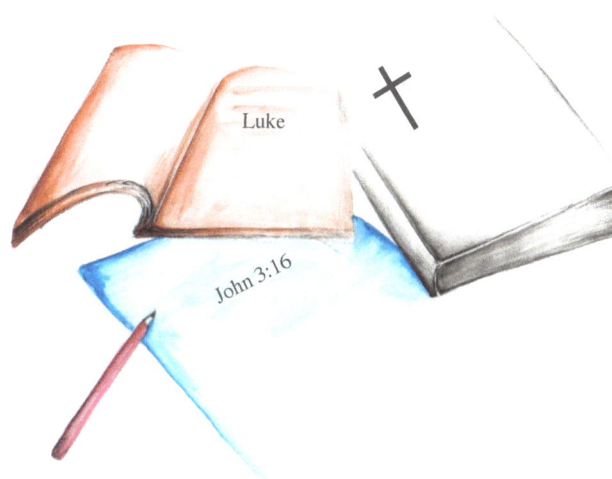

Chapter 1

A Teacher is a Minister, Salesman, and Visionary Leader

It is the glory of God to conceal a thing: but the honor of kings (and teachers) is to search out a matter. **(Proverbs 25:2)**

Your role is to teach, to advise, and to persuade your class members to become like Christ. Your goals require natural talent and supernatural anointing.

You are a Minister

You want more for your class than merely knowing **about** God, you want them to *experience* him. Therefore, in addition to teaching the scriptures, you want to minister to your students. Allocating time for praise reports, prayer, and testimonies are all wonderful ways to minister to one another. Singing is also a way to invite the Lord's presence into your classroom. In these practical ways, the class will see God at work from week to week as prayers are answered. They not only become more knowledgeable, they gain first-hand experience in walking with God. Students' gifts will emerge during these times of testimony. This heart-to-heart sharing with one another and communion with God transforms your class into a ministry. In fact, if your class is one hour long, you should not teach more than 40 minutes, because you'll need ten minutes at the start and close for greetings, fellowship and prayer requests. If it weren't for fellowship, your students could simply stay home and study the Bible through correspondence courses. Making time for relationships strengthens the Christian body through emotional support, accountability, and service.

Through practical in-class ministry, students learn to bear one another's burdens, and carry the concerns of their friends to the Lord in prayer. They also go beyond asking for blessings to **seek the Blesser**; beyond asking for healing, to seek the Healer. Ministering to one another creates Christ-likeness.

We are to be "doers of the word, and not hearers only." (James 1:22) Many Christians already know more about the Christian life than they are putting into practice.

You Are a Salesperson

A good salesperson likes to create drama and enjoys the suspense of influencing others. You are persuading all the time, for good or not, by your credibility, attitude, and character. You are the most compelling visual aid that your students will see. But remember that you are never alone on the teaching platform because you are a coworker with God. Lastly, keep in mind that persuasion takes time. Although you should expect progress, the length of time required is in God's hands. *"By long forbearing is a prince persuaded, and a soft tongue breaks the bone."* (Proverbs 25:15)

Verbal skill is helpful. Proverbs 16:21 tells us, *"A wise, mature man is known for his understanding. The more pleasant his words, the more persuasive he is."* Frame your lessons in language that is tasty and wholesome. *"When a wise man speaks, he makes knowledge attractive."* (Proverbs 15:2). Ephesians 4:15 tells us to speak the truth in love. And Proverbs 15:4 says that kind words bring life.

A good teacher not only conveys information, but also expresses care. They don't care how much you know until they know how much you care.

You Are a Visionary Leader

From the very beginning, a visionary leader knows what the project is supposed to look like in the end. Although Peter did not see himself as the chief apostle, the Lord did. Paul did not see himself as a great evangelist, but Jesus did. Mary Magdalene saw herself as a castoff, but the Savior saw what she could become: a person of courage, faith, and love. Pray about the direction of your class and the needs of its members. God has placed you there to develop them.

Jesus inspired his disciples by sharing his vision for them as "fishers of men." God's vision for all of our lives is always much bigger than our own.

You have a huge responsibility and a great opportunity. Your *"lips should flow with the knowledge of God so the people will learn God's laws."* (Malachi 2:7, TLB)

Chapter 2

The Blessings of Being a Teacher

I count all things but loss for the excellency of the knowledge of Christ Jesus my Lord. (Philippians 3:8)

The greatest benefit of being a teacher is increased insight in becoming more like Jesus Christ. You have the unparalleled gift of studying God's revealed truth, the Scriptures. There is nothing that compares to the Bible.

- **The Word was with God at creation.**
  In the beginning was the Word. (John 1:1)
- **The Word is God.**
  The Word was God. (John 1:1)
- **The Word is Jesus.**
  And the Word was made flesh, and dwelt among us. (John 1:14)

It is not enough to say that the Bible tells us **about** Jesus: **the Bible is Jesus!** Studying and applying the Scripture is an awesome honor and privilege!

Be joyful that it is *"your Father's good pleasure to give you the kingdom."* (Luke 12:32) You are following in the footsteps of Jesus, the greatest teacher, King Solomon, the wisest man, and Paul, the Apostle. Before his ascension, Jesus asked Peter the question that qualifies you for being a teacher, *"Love me more than these?"* Jesus needs teachers who love him more than anyone else, more than anything else, and more than their own lives. If you answer with the confidence of Peter, *"Yes, Lord; you know that I love you,"* then, and only then, will you receive his command: *"Feed my lambs."* (John 21:15) Don't be cold-hearted, the hard-hearted, or the half-hearted.

Kindness and Peace

"Do you want more and more of God's kindness and peace? **Then learn to know him better and better.** *For as you know him better, he will give you, through his great power, everything you need for living a truly good life: he even shares his own glory and his own goodness with us!"* (2 Peter 1:2,3, The Living Bible)

Eternal Honor

Billy Graham's Sunday School teachers could not have known the great impact that he would later have, but they contributed to his success and will receive a reward like his. Jesus said, *"If you welcome a prophet because he is a man of God, you will be given the same reward a prophet gets."* (Matthew 10:41, TLB) Bible teacher, there is a permanent, glorious reward waiting for you in heaven. Eternity will prove that Sunday School was a great and worthy service for God.

- *The reapers will be paid good wages and will be gathering eternal souls into the granaries of heaven! What joys await the sower and the reaper, both together!* (John 4:36, TLB)

- *Whosoever therefore shall break one of these least commandments, and shall teach men so, he shall be called the least in the kingdom of heaven:* **but whosoever shall do and teach them, the same shall be called great in the kingdom of heaven.** (Matthew 5:19)

- *And they that be wise shall shine as the brightness of the firmament; and they that turn many to righteousness as the stars for ever and ever.* (Daniel 12:3)

Earthly Honor

*"Let the elders that rule well be counted worthy of double honor, **especially they who labor in the word and doctrine.**"* (1 Timothy 5:17) The church depends upon teachers to bring out the wonders of **SCRIPTURE** skillfully. Your fellow Christians know how much time it takes to be a good Sunday School teacher. They also recognize that God has given you a gift and that you live close to the Lord. Psalm 25:14 tells us that *"The secret of the Lord is with those who fear Him."* This means that God shares his thoughts with you and you are familiar with matters of faith. You are a custodian of God's riches.

Henceforth I call you not servants; for the servant knows not what his lord does: but I have called you friends; for all things that I have heard of my Father I have made known unto you. (John 15:15) You are a close friend of the Lord.

Would you rather be anywhere else?
Would you rather do anything else?

The Very Presence of the Lord

Teaching them to observe all things whatsoever I have commanded you:
*and, lo, **I am with you** always, even unto the end of the world. Amen.* (Matthew 28:20)

Isn't it encouraging to know that Jesus is right there with us as we teach?

I will never leave you, nor forsake you. (Hebrews 13:5)

You don't have to teach alone.

Chapter 3

Don't Teach Without These 10 Things
Be thou prepared. (Ezekiel 38:7)

1. The gift of teaching.

Teaching without the gift of teaching is like placing a pack horse in the Kentucky Derby. It just doesn't look right. Psalms 127:1 *"Except the Lord build the house, they labor in vain that build it."*

To someone not gifted for the classroom, teaching can be unpleasant and burdensome. However, if you're a teacher, you like a lively debate, a thoughtful question, and interaction with your class. Mixing it up with your students is fun. It's what makes you a teacher.

It is important that you minister in your gift. Second Timothy 1:6 tells us to *"stir up the gift of God."* When we operate in our gift, we teach with confidence, not arrogance. Like the prophet Habakkuk, we say *"The Lord God is my strength."*

A good Bible teacher is also a good Bible student, so you will enjoy studying the scriptures and becoming thoroughly familiar with them. You will delight in your own walk in Christ and learning more about God's will. And when God reveals something powerful in the scriptures, you will want to share it. You will also have a desire to see others grow into mature, strong Christians. In short, you will want to do your best to help others: and continuing your own Christian education keeps you sharp. *"When you stop learning, you will soon neglect what you already know."* (Proverbs 19:27, TEV)

2. An understanding that God expects more from you.

God holds teachers to a higher standard than others. James 3:1 tells us *"Dear brothers, don't be too eager to tell others their faults, for we all make many mistakes; and **when we teachers** of religion, who should know better, do wrong, our punishment will be **greater than it would be for others**.* Luke 12:48 reinforces this admonition: *Much is required from those to whom much is given, for **their responsibility is greater**.*

Maintain a godly life. Although your salvation may not be at stake, your eternal rewards are. Pray that God will give you the wisdom, strength, and faith to live a clean life: *"worthy of those who have been chosen for such wonderful blessings as these."* (Ephesians 4:1, The Living Bible)

The Lord warns us in Jeremiah 23:1 *"Woe be unto the pastors that destroy and scatter the sheep of my pasture!"* Ezekiel 34:2 says *"Woe to the shepherds who feed themselves instead of their flocks."*

3. A realization that your life speaks louder than your words.

"I have heard of you by the hearing of the ear, but now my eye sees you." Job 42:5
I once traveled a great distance to attend a seminar for Christian men. Although I was impressed by the effort, organization and lectures at the church, I noticed a few of the key leaders failed to apply their own lessons. They spoke of having a humble heart, yet exhibited a self-centered attitude. This discouraged me from attending future training there.

From the book of Judges, we learn that people require leadership that they can see. Each time a judge died in Israel, the Israelites reverted to their old sinful ways. Without visible examples, people turn away from God. If you don't live the truths you espouse, your credibility will suffer. *At the end of the day, the life you lead is the real Bible lesson.*

4. God's anointing. What is the anointing?

Dr. Harold Hunter, the admired President of Trinity Theological Seminary, defines the anointing as:
"A special touch of God to do a special task at a special time in your life."

- The anointing will allow you to comfortably perform the ministry to which you are called.
- The anointing will enable you to do what others cannot. In other words, your ministry will work.
- As you minister, people will recognize the anointing.

The anointing occurs when God places his Spirit upon you for a certain purpose. In Luke 4:18, Jesus said, *"The Spirit of the Lord is upon me, because he has anointed me to preach the gospel to the poor."* The anointing is God's spiritual blessing of liberty, authority and power. Ask for God's blessing to bring freedom to you as you teach. Remember, *"where the Spirit of the Lord is, there is liberty."* (2 Corinthians 3:17) Teaching under the anointing is different than teaching for God: it is God teaching **through you**.

If you are to demonstrate Christ to your students, you need God's commission, affirmation, and enablement for teaching. If Jesus needed God's divine touch, surely you do also: *"**God anointed Jesus** of Nazareth with the Holy Ghost and with power."* (Acts 10:38) Jesus is known as "The Christ," which means "The Anointed." **Jesus spoke only the words which God gave him**. (John 17:8) Listen to his astounding words: *"The words that I speak to you I do not speak on My own authority; but the Father who dwells in Me does the works."* (John 14:10, NKJV)

The apostle Paul spoke of God's anointing of Silvanus, Timothy and himself as preachers of the gospel: *"Now He who establishes us with you in Christ and **has anointed us** is God."* (2 Corinthians 1:21) Like Timothy, we should seek the anointing of God to teach. The anointing brings the truth to life. It is the Spirit to Spirit connection from God to us.

A review of the Bible tells us that the anointing brings great and wonderful blessings:

- God's approval (Matthew 3:16)
- Crowning, signifying royalty (Leviticus 21:12)
- Respect (Exodus 30:30, 31)
- Formal consecration and declaration of ordination for ministry (Acts 13:3)
- Honor as holy and godly (Exodus 30:30)
- Sanctification, or being set apart for a specific ministry (Leviticus 8:12)
- Placing of responsibility on a minister (Numbers 18:8)
- Preparation and beautification (Isaiah 21:5)
- A sign of affection and care (John 12:3)
- ***Bestowing of a fragrant aroma (John 12:3)***
- Establishment (2 Corinthians 1:21)
- Deliverance and victory (Isaiah 10:27)
- The Holy Ghost and power (Acts 10:38)

5. A caring heart.

The primary motivation for teaching is caring. You don't teach to be admired or to demonstrate your public speaking abilities. Students do not remember the wittiest, most theatrical or the most educated teachers. They cherish the teachers who took a personal interest in them and spent time with them. You will have the greatest and most lasting impact on them if you are available at crucial times when they need you. These moments are not always scheduled: they occur unexpectedly. Because ministering is the more important half of teaching, be willing to interrupt the lesson to pray for someone or speak a word of encouragement to him. TIME is an acronym for "**T**aking **I**nterest in **ME**."

Consider Paul, the author of much of the New Testament and founder of many churches. The scars on his back from five brutal whippings displayed his devotion to the early Christians. Yet, he called his suffering a *"light affliction."* (2 Corinthians 4:17)

Also note that King Solomon recorded his wise sayings out of compassion for his people. Solomon gave special care to word his proverbs in a pleasing manner, so that his readers would *enjoy* becoming wise. *"But then, because the Preacher was wise, he went on teaching the people all he knew; and he collected proverbs and classified them. For the Preacher was not only a wise man, but a good teacher; he not only taught what he knew to the people, but taught them in an interesting manner."* (Ecclesiastes 12:9-12, The Living Bible) **He cared enough to make learning enjoyable.**

People need to know someone cares. When the Israelites were slaves in a foreign land, the Lord said, *I know their sorrows.*" (Exodus 3:7)

The Greek translation of teach is "paratithemi," which means "to set before." It connotes placing a nourishing meal in front of someone.

Do you recognize the great need? Do you care enough to prepare wholesome, spiritual food for them? Are you available?

6. Passion for the Bible.

Passion is the difference between a good teacher and a great teacher. It is a gift of God and a matter of the heart. If you want to know God's word, you will immerse yourself in scripture. Love for scripture is a must because *"A good man **out of the good treasure of his heart** brings forth that which is good."* (Luke 6:45)
David proclaimed:
> *I have rejoiced in the way of **your testimonies**, as much as in all riches.*
> *I will meditate in **your precepts**, and have respect unto your ways.*
> *I will delight myself in **your statutes**: I will not forget your word.* (Psalm 119:14-16)

Jesus declared, *"the words that I speak unto you, they are spirit, and they are life."* (John 6:63) The Scriptures have universal, across-the-board impact in every area of our lives. *All scripture is given by inspiration of God, and is profitable for doctrine, for reproof, for correction, for instruction in righteousness: That the man of God may be perfect, thoroughly furnished unto all good works.* (2 Timothy 3:16-17) The Bible says "**all**" good works, meaning social, political, family, recreational, and economic activities. It is not restricted to spiritual matters. You don't *spend* time studying, you *invest* it.

Nothing great was ever accomplished without enthusiasm. If you have a passion for the Bible, an hour reading scriptures will seem like 30 minutes. Remember, preparing a Bible lesson is too demanding if you don't enjoy it.

7. Physical Well Being.

Public speaking demands energy. In order to maintain your health and enthusiasm, exercise, rest and eat wisely!

8. An understanding of the cost.

<u>Don't start anything you can't soak in prayer.</u> Teaching requires prayer, study, thought, preparation, and administrative work. Unless you have time each week to pray for your class members, the lesson, and for wisdom, don't accept a teaching assignment. This means dropping some other time-consuming activity to make room for prayer time. King Solomon, who was famous for his wisdom, warned against becoming overcommitted: *"being too busy gives you nightmares."* (Ecclesiastes 5:3 TLB) The cause of stress is being torn in too many directions. It is cumulative; lots of little things piling up.

In Luke 14:28-29, Jesus cautioned against committing yourself without full knowledge of the demands of what you are getting into: *"For which of you, intending to build a tower, sits not down first, and counts the cost, whether he have sufficient to finish it? Lest haply, after he has laid the foundation, and is not able to finish it, all that behold it begin to mock him."*

9. Desire to change students into teachers.

Some teachers believe their mission is to grow a bigger class for themselves. However, there is no success without a successor. Ultimately, you want other Bible studies to emerge from your class.

A wonderful way to develop a student into a teacher is by allowing him to substitute for you. You will be away at some time during the year, so identify several good men from your class who are willing to fill in. Follow Paul's guidance to pass on the torch: *"And the things that you have heard of me among many witnesses, the same commit to faithful men, who shall be able to teach others also."*
(2 Timothy 2:2) Notice that Paul said **"faithful"** men. Given time and practice, they **"shall be able"** to teach. You can make a good man able, but you can't make an able man good.

10. Time to pray for your class.

As you approach your teaching assignment, have an attitude of dependence upon God. Jesus said, *"without Me you can do nothing."* (John 15:5 NKJV) With this perspective, we are compelled to bring our lesson, our students, and ourselves before God in prayer, asking for his blessing. We should also thank God in advance for the good work that he will do. *"Be careful for nothing; but **in every thing by prayer and supplication with thanksgiving** let your requests be made known unto God."* (Philippians 4:6)

Summary
If you:

- have the gift of teaching
- naturally care enough to be devoted to your class.
- know you need God's anointing each week.
- are living a godly life.
- are willing to be held to a higher standard.
- enjoy the drama and excitement of the classroom.
- have a passion for his holy Word.
- have evaluated the time and effort required.
- are willing to saturate your class in prayer.
- have confidence that you know what needs to be taught.

Then, teach!

Your best is good enough.

Chapter 4

The Personal Life of the Teacher

The secret of the Lord is with those that fear Him, and he will show them His covenant. Psalm 25:14, NKJV

Genius is being able to keep things on track. Keeping your life clean is essential. Your ministry is the overflow of your personal devotional life. Please note that Paul said that he was teaching **more than the gospel**, he was pouring *out his own soul* to them, *"being affectionately desirous of you, we were willing to have imparted unto you, not the gospel of God only, but also **our own souls**, because you were dear unto us."* (1 Thessalonians 2:7-8) When you teach, you will be pouring out your personality to your church family. Because of this, you should be loving and sincere. Students can see through a hypocrite.

The Bible tells us that Paul had to confront Peter about not living the life he was teaching: *"But when Peter was come to Antioch, I withstood him to the face, because he was to be blamed.* (Galatians 2:11) We need to be consistent, both in and out of the classroom. In Ephesians 4:1, Paul exhorts us to *"walk worthy of the vocation where you are called."*

Sexual Purity

The great evangelist Billy Graham said no one could ever be a dynamic Christian without sexually purity. As a teacher, you don't want anything to diminish your spiritual power.

Teaching is for tough hombres

Teaching is not for sissies. It requires Christians who are strong in faith and faithful in obedience. In his letter to Timothy, the apostle compared teachers to combat soldiers who do not allow themselves to be bogged down by business or favorite hobbies.

"Endure hardness, as a good soldier of Jesus Christ. No man that wars entangles himself with the affairs of this life; that he may please him who has chosen him to be a soldier." (2 Timothy 2:3, 4)

You can maintain your freshness if you focus on your **vertical** relationship with God. Those who burn out have been living for the approval of others, their **horizontal** relationships.

Little prayer gives little power.
Some prayer give some power.
Much prayer gives much power.

Take the following precautions against these enemies of integrity.

1. **TEMPTATION.** Temptation is losing focus. One defense against temptation is your regular morning quiet time of prayer. Pray Psalms 139:23-24: *"Search me, O God, and know my heart: try me, and know my thoughts: And see if there be any wicked way in me, and lead me in the way everlasting."* Fully realize that your ministry is at risk through temptation.

2. **STRESS.** Stress comes from being pulled in too many directions. Simplify your life and refocus on the ministry God has given you.

3. **FATIGUE.** Fatigue is cumulative and can be described as "battle fatigue." We cannot let our guard down. Fighters who drop even one hand get hit.
   (a) **For mental conditioning**: Read the Bible and listen to Christian teaching. Teach on topics that excite you. *"A relaxed attitude lengthens a man's life"* (Proverbs 14:30)
   (b) **For physical well-being**: Diet, exercise, and rest. Take a break and enjoy a change of scenery, especially after a great expenditure of your time and energy. Follow the Lord's example, who *"often withdrew into the wilderness and prayed."* (Luke 6:16, NKJV). Also, remember to observe the day of rest each week. Sometimes, the most spiritual thing you can do is rest.
   (c) **For spiritual strength**. Worship and praise God, because he inhabits the praises of Israel. (Psalm 22:3)
   (d) **For relational wholeness**. Fellowship with other godly Christians who will pray for you.

4. **UNREALISTIC DEMANDS of OTHERS** (peer pressure). Don't be afraid to have and express feelings, including sadness and anger. Anger held in becomes depression. *"Open rebuke is better than secret love."* (Proverbs 27:5)

5. **FEAR OF FAILURE.** Few things in life are irreversible. Be decisive in following God and leave the outcome to him.

6. **FEAR OF BURNING OUT.** Although it would be stupid to run ourselves into the ground, it is easier to "rust out" than to burn out. With reasonable care and rest, you can keep up the good work. Realize that your ministry is critical and that without quality teachers, the family of God will stumble. Answer the need of the hour with David's compelling question: *"Is there not a cause?"* (1 Samuel 17:29)

7. **DESIRE for SELF-PRESERVATION.** Avoiding rejection should not be your goal. "Woe unto you, when all me shall speak well of you!" (Luke 6:26) Don't take rejection personally. *"He who rejects this does not reject man, but God."* (1 Thessalonians 4:8, NKJ) *Reject rejection.*

8. **IDLENESS.** Idleness is being unproductive. It comes from losing communion with Jesus. Often such disconnection comes from the internet, television, and recycled news shown over and over. Don't waste time.

9. **REPUTATION-BUILDING.** It is okay to rock the boat once in a while. Sometimes, emotion and anger are appropriate. Our attitude should be that of John the Baptist, who said, *"He (Jesus) must become greater and greater, and I must become less and less."* (John 3:30, TLB)

Chapter 5

Why They Come to Class and How This Can Help You

A friendly discussion is as stimulating as the sparks that fly when iron strikes iron. (Proverbs 27:17, TLB)

Ninety percent of people come to Bible class to enjoy their friends. Although your own attendance may have always been to learn something, most people come for fellowship.

This is why the traditional 10 minutes at the start of class is critical: class members have an opportunity to greet and visit with one another. Furthermore, in the opening minutes of class, it is important to allocate time for prayer and praise.

This desire to interact with the others in the group is a good thing and can be used to your advantage. Don't limit their interpersonal contributions to the beginning of class. Draw them into the presentation. Call on willing class members to answer questions, share their experiences and read scripture. Your students have valuable input that will energize your class much more than if you simply lectured the entire period.

Remember the three secrets to a happy class:
- **class participation**
- **class participation**
- **class participation.**

21 ways to get Class Members involved:

1. Ask if anyone has a testimony or a praise report.

2. Ask someone to lead the opening prayer.

3. Ask if "anyone" would like to read the Scripture. (This is preferable to asking someone by name without advance notice because not everyone is comfortable reading aloud).

4. Ask how they would feel if they were going through circumstances such as the Bible character you are studying.

5. Ask if they have ever gone through similar circumstances and how it turned out.

6. Ask them why God allowed the events you are studying.

7. Ask what they would pray for if they were a character in your Bible lesson.

8. Ask if they have ever known anyone like the Bible character you are studying.

9. Ask if they know anyone who exhibits the qualities you are studying. And ask what impact the person had on the people around him or her.

10. Ask them to rank, from most important to least important, qualities you are studying. And ask why they rated them as they did. (Ranking qualities, and events, is a great activity for small break out groups because it reveals their values).

11. Ask them how they think **God** would rank the qualities you are studying.

12. Ask them if they have any of the qualities we reviewed today. Which ones?

13. Ask how much responsibility they have for their own spiritual growth.

14. Have class members role play where one is a news reporter and the other is the Biblical character from the lesson.

15. Ask what stages or phases the Biblical character went through in your study.

16. Have the class identify the traps or obstacles that could have caused the failure of the main character. Do these same pitfalls exist today? How would you avoid them?

17. Ask if success in this area of Christian life is a result of brain power. Faith? Obedience?

18. Ask what expectations God has for them and if they expect a test in this area.

19. Ask them if they believe God is in a rush to develop them spiritually.

20. Ask them to list specific ways they can apply the things they learned today.

21. Ask if they are willing to pursue God's design for their lives even if no one around them offers support.

Chapter 6

Seeing the Person Your Student Will Become

What's more, I am changing your name. It will no longer be Abram. Instead, you will be called Abraham, for you will be the Father of many nations. (Genesis 17:5)

In Psalms 139, we learn that God saw our substance before we were formed. *"Your eyes saw my substance, being yet unformed."* "Substance," in the original Greek, means "standing under." It is the original, undiluted ingredient that composes all that you are.

As a teacher, you are also called to see the essential composition of your students: who they are deep inside. Bring out this unique creation! The student that you see with your eyes should be much different than the student you envision in your spirit.

Jesus looked at local fishermen and beheld international evangelists. God saw a cautious farmer named Gideon, but envisioned a daring military leader. The Lord observed an enemy called Saul, but brought forth a pastor named Paul.

An ounce of solid gold is often surrounded by tons of dirt, and it takes someone with perception and persistence to uncover it. So it is with teachers and students. Your students may come to you with little Bible knowledge or experience in the Christian life. After pouring yourself into them, you can become frustrated if you don't see immediate results. Remember that things take time. What if the Lord had ended teaching his disciples because of their slow progress? He could have simply walked away. Yet the Lord devoted himself to his disciples and endured much frustration before he saw any evidence that they would become the great figures of the first century. Jesus wasn't looking for the dirt, he was looking for the pure gold underneath.

Like the farmer in Mark 4, we need to wait patiently for the harvest. *So is the kingdom of God, as if a man should cast seed into the ground; And should sleep, and rise night and day, and the seed should spring and grow up, he knows not how. For the earth brings forth fruit of herself;* **first the blade, then the ear, after that the full corn in the ear.**

The fact that they are coming to Bible class at all is encouraging. Obviously, your class is voluntary and they could have chosen to stay home. Remember that each and every student has at least one unique gift that you can cultivate for the Kingdom of God. *"Every man has his proper gift of God, one after this manner, and another after that."* (1 Corinthians 7:7) Each student is ***"fearfully and wonderfully made."***

How can you recognize God's plan for your student?

By observing a student's interests and how he invests his time, you can identify his natural gifting. His own preferences are the most likely indicator of his future role in the Kingdom of God. For example, God placed a passion in Nehemiah's heart to restore his home city of Jerusalem. (Nehemiah 2:12) The king could tell that Nehemiah had a burden by his demeanor and countenance. Likewise, you can recognize a student's interests by his expressions, words, and actions. If he brings guests to class, he may have a burden for souls. If he enjoys helping with the chairs, offering, and role call, he may have the gift of helping. (1 Corinthians 12:28)

When you identify a student's interests, you can find common ground on which to build a relationship. Paul said *"To the weak became I as weak, that I might gain the weak: I am made all things to all men, that I might by all means save some."* (1 Corinthians 9:22) These commonalities you have with your students provide an opportunity to establish relationships. As an experienced teacher, you can then build on the knowledge and zeal that a student already displays, and channel this into service for God. Upon finding a motivated student, the natural and right thing to do is to teach more, for *"unto every one which has shall be given."* (Luke 19:26)

Pray for God to give you special insight into your students. When Jesus recruited Nathanael, the Lord's knowledge of his character awed him, and the promise of great things ahead thrilled him: *"Jesus saw Nathanael coming to him, and said of him,* **Behold an Israelite indeed, in whom is no guile!** *Nathanael said unto him, Whence knew you me? Jesus answered and said unto him, Before that Philip called you, when you were under the fig tree, I saw you. Nathanael answered and said unto him, Rabbi, you are the Son of God; you are the King of Israel. Jesus answered and said unto him, Because I said unto you, I saw you under the fig tree, believed you?* **You shall see greater things than these."** (John 1:47-50)

Jesus had a vision of his disciples and so should you. He knew how significant they could become in God's Kingdom. You know what a mature Christian looks like. Do not let a little frustration cause you to lose your vision for the future.

At the right time, share your vision with them, as Jesus did with Peter. "You are Peter, and upon this rock I will build my church." (Matthew 16:18)

The top three key ingredients for a relationship are:

     1. time
     2. time
     3. time

To students, TIME stands for *"Taking an Interest in Me"*.

Chapter 7

First Things First: Spiritual Warfare

*And the evil spirit answered and said, "Jesus I know, and Paul I know; but **who are you**?"* (Acts 19:15)

1. Who Are You?

As a Christian, you are a:

✦ **Royal priest.**
*But you are a chosen generation, **a royal priesthood,** a holy nation, His own special people.* (1 Peter 2:9, NKJV)

✦ **King and a priest unto God.**
*And has made us **kings and priests** unto God and his Father.* (Revelation 1:6)

✦ **Member of the family of God.**
*For whom he did foreknow, he also did predestinate to be conformed to the image of his Son, that he might be the firstborn **among many brethren.*** (Romans 8:29) Christians, *"being many, are one body in Christ, and every one members one of another."* (Romans 12:5)

2. What Does This Mean Regarding Spiritual Warfare?

✦ **Because of your relationship to Jesus Christ, you have complete authority over demons.**
In Luke 10:19-20, Jesus said *"Behold, I give unto you power to tread on serpents and scorpions, and over all the power of the enemy: and nothing shall by any means hurt you. Notwithstanding in this rejoice not, that the spirits are subject unto you; but rather rejoice, **because your names are written in heaven.**"* You are a member of the holy, royal, ruling family of God, who has *"raised us up together, and made us sit together in the heavenly places in Christ Jesus."* (Ephesians 2:6) As "kings and priests unto God," we are in the chain of command of heaven. Our job is to maintain the order established by Christ; namely, to keep Satan under our feet. Demons know that you have authority over them and they must obey your royal commands. Rest assured of your dominion and authority as a Christian.

✦ **You are backed by the full authority of heaven.** *Assuredly, I say to you, whatever you bind (restrict) on earth will be bound in heaven, and whatever you loose (dissolve) on earth will be loosed in heaven.* (Matthew 18:18, NKJV)

3. Satan Will Attend Your Class If Not Prevented

✦ **Satan would like to infiltrate the church.** We know this from Mark 1:23: *"And there was **in their synagogue** a man with an unclean spirit."* Demons want to destroy ministries and the fellowship of believers. This is not a strange thing: David, Peter, Paul, and John all encountered demons.

✦ **Satan is free to attend your class unless you or God prevents him.** Jesus said there is no way to take Satan's possessions until you bind him **first**. Jesus said *"first;"* before anything else takes place. *"Or else how can one enter into a strong man's (the devil's) house, and spoil his goods, except he **first** bind the strong man? And then he will spoil his house."* (Matthew 12:29)

✦ **How do you bind (restrict) the devil from your class?** You stop his activity the same way Jesus did: **by your verbal command**. *"Then **said Jesus unto him, Get you hence, Satan.**"* (Matthew 4:10) Jesus went on to quote scripture. James 4:7 tells us to "resist the devil, and he will flee from you." So, command the devil *in the name (the authority) of Jesus Christ* to stay off the church grounds and order him not to return or retaliate. Take preventive measures against him. When your class is secure, you will know it in your spirit. You are then ready to pray to receive God's unhindered blessings.

✦ **Jesus told us that banished devils would like to return:** *"When an unclean spirit goes out of a man (or a class), he goes through dry places, seeking rest, and finds none. Then he says, 'I will return to my house from which I came.'"* (Matthew 12:43-44). Command Satan that he cannot return or retaliate.

4. Who Satan Is and What He Does

✦ **Satan is an angel who rebelled against God.** Although once *"the anointed cherub"* and *"perfect in (his) ways,"* *"iniquity was found in (him)."* Thus God pronounced judgment against him: *"Your heart was lifted up because of your beauty; You corrupted your wisdom for the sake of your splendor; **I cast you to the ground**.* (Ezekiel 28:14 and 17) *"Your pomp is brought down to the grave, and the noise of your viols: the worm is spread under you, and the worms cover you. How are you fallen from heaven, O Lucifer, son of the morning! **How are you cut down to the ground,** which did weaken the nations! For you have said in your heart, I will ascend into heaven, I will exalt my throne above the stars of God: I will sit also upon the mount of the congregation, in the sides of the north: I will ascend above the heights of the clouds; I will be like the most High."* Swept away by his own glory, this created angel became God's defiant enemy when he tried to take God's place.

✦ **A minority of angels joined Satan in his rebellion.** Revelation 12:4 tells us that the dragon took one-third *"of the stars of heaven, and did cast them to the earth."* This refers to *"the angels which kept not their first estate, but left their own habitation."* (Jude 1:6) Some of these former angels, now demons, are organized by Satan against God and his people.

I compare demons to remnant defeated Civil War veterans who, after the fall of the Confederacy, continued to raid the countryside. They were still organized and malicious, but they had no legal authority whatsoever. And just as the conquered Confederacy had no right to rule any longer, Satan has no right to afflict Christians. Therefore, we should not give the devil any justification to enter our lives, such as sin, unforgiveness, or bitterness. In other words, don't leave him any open doors.

One day, the devil and his demons will all be *"cast alive into a lake of fire burning with brimstone"* where they *"shall be tormented day and night for ever and ever."* (Revelation 19:20 and 20:10). For now, we should: *"Be sober, be vigilant; because your adversary the devil, as a roaring lion, walks about, seeking whom he may devour."* (1 Peter 5:8)

✦ **Jesus referred to Satan as "a murderer" and "a liar" and "the wicked one."** *He was a **murderer** from the beginning, and abode not in the truth, because there is no truth in him. When he speaks a lie, he speaks of his own: for he is a **liar**, and the father of it."* (John 8:44) *He answered and said unto them, He that sows the good seed is the Son of man; The field is the world; the good seed are the children of the kingdom; but the tares are the children of **the wicked one**; The enemy that sowed them is the devil.* (Matthew 13:37-39) It is humanly impossible to understand the consuming hatred that Satan has for us. Jesus called him *"**the** enemy,"* not an enemy. Satan wants the very worst for you.

✦ **Satan steals, kills, and destroys.** *"The thief comes not, but for to steal, and to kill, and to destroy: I am come that they might have life, and that they might have it more abundantly."* (John 10:10) Satan has only three objectives: to steal (everything), to kill (everyone), to destroy (all creation).

First Things First: Spiritual Warfare

✦ **Most people are members of Satan's family and slaves to his will.** Most people are servants of the devil. They are his servants because they have voluntarily submitted to him. Paul explained this relationship: *"Do you realize that you can choose your own master? You can choose sin (with death) or else obedience (with acquittal). The one to whom you offer yourself-he will take you and be your master and you will be his slave."* (Romans 6:16) Peter said, *"of whom a man is overcome (the devil), of the same is he brought in bondage."* (2 Peter 2:19)

5. Jesus Has Defeated Satan and Removed His Authority.

How did Jesus overthrow Satan's authority and take his power? Just before Jesus' sacrifice on the cross, Jesus declared *"now shall the prince of this world (the devil) be cast out."* (John 12:31). In Luke 10:18, Jesus said, *"I beheld Satan as lightning fall from heaven."* By his death and resurrection, Jesus overthrew Satan and the power of sin irreversibly and forever. Because of this, *"God raised him up to the heights of heaven and gave him a name which is **above every other name**, that at the name of Jesus every knee shall bow in heaven and on earth and under the earth."* (Philippians 2: 9, 10) We have a new ruler now, Jesus Christ whose name (authority) is **high above** all other names (authorities). *"**Far above** all principality, and power, and might, and dominion, and every name that is named, not only in this world, but also in that which is to come: And has put **all things under his feet**, and gave him to be the head over all things.* (Ephesians 1:21, 22) That is why Jesus said: *"All power is given unto me in heaven and in earth."* (Matthew 28:18)

6. Jesus Has Given You Authority and He Expects You to Use It.

✦ The Lord has delegated his authority to you. Jesus said, *Behold, I give unto **you** power to tread on serpents and scorpions, and over **all** the power of the enemy: and nothing shall by any means hurt you.* (Luke 10:19-20)

✦ Jesus foretold that Christians would cast out demons. *In my name shall they cast out devils.* (Mark 16:17)

✦ Luke 10:17 documents the submission of demons to Christians. *And the seventy returned again with joy, saying, Lord, even the devils are subject unto us **through thy name.*** (through Jesus' authority)

✦ Acts 16:18 describes the submission of a demon. Paul also demonstrated this authority over Satan and his demons. *But Paul, being grieved, turned and **said to the spirit,** I command you **in the name of Jesus Christ** (with the authority of Jesus) to come out of her. And he came out the same hour.* (Acts 16:18) As an authorized representative of the Lord, Paul exercised the authority of Christ over the evil spirit by **commanding** him to leave.

✦ **We, his church, should take the offensive against Satan and overpower him:** Jesus said, *I will build my church; and the gates of hell shall not prevail against it. And I will give unto you the keys of the kingdom of heaven: and whatsoever you shall bind on earth shall be bound in heaven: and whatsoever thou shalt loose on earth shall be loosed in heaven.* (Matthew 16:18,19) These verses tell us that whatsoever (evil spirits) we bind, or restrict, on earth will have already been bound in heaven. And whatsoever chains we dissolve on earth will have already been dissolved in heaven. We have the support and backing of Heaven!

7. After you have bound the devil, decree God's blessings upon your class.

It is important to speak positively, thankfully declaring and decreeing God's blessings and favor over your students; and asking his blessings of wisdom upon your class.

✦ **Proclaim the blessings of the Lord.** *"Let the redeemed of the Lord say so."* (Psalms 107:2) Declare his goodness. *"You shall also* **decree a thing***, and it shall be established unto you: and the light shall shine upon your ways."* (Job 22:28) You are a royal priest, so decree and declare good things for your class, such as Ephesians 1:17: *"That the God of our Lord Jesus Christ, the Father of glory, may give unto you (your students) the spirit of wisdom and revelation in the knowledge of him."*

✦ **Plead with the Lord to cover you and your class with his blood.** When you declare the blood of Jesus, you are proclaiming all the forgiveness, all the right standing, all the power, all the healing, all the protection, all the blessings, and all the authority won by Jesus at Calvary. Pray for God to control every comment, thought, prayer, and deed in your class. Invite his presence and blessings.

Chapter 8

Paul's Pattern for Presentations

Join in following my example … you have us for a pattern…
(Philippians 3:17)

An examination of Paul's letters reveals a consistent pattern he followed in teaching. Paul's format appears in Romans, First and Second Corinthians, Ephesians, Philippians, and Colossians.

1. INTRODUCTION. Introduce yourself and let the class know how long you have been teaching as well as any pertinent information about yourself or the series of lessons you are covering. For example, you might tell the class how long you have been a member of the church.

2. GREETING. Paul always offered a heartfelt greeting to his beloved congregation. Give a warm welcome to your class. He also states his affection for them and tells them that he has been praying for them.

3. BLESSING. Paul's blessing in both Romans and 1 Corinthians is, *Grace to you and peace from God our Father and the Lord Jesus Christ.*

4. GOOD WORD. Prayer and praise reports are a ***great*** way to begin. Psalm 100:4 tells us to *Enter into his gates with thanksgiving, and into his courts with praise.* Many examples abound in scripture: Romans 1:8, 1 Corinthians 1:4-6; 2 Corinthians 1:11, Ephesians 1:15, and Philippians 1:3-7. Paul complimented the Romans on their faith; the Corinthians for their knowledge, testimony, and gifts; the Ephesians for their fellowship with him and their participation in the defense of the gospel. **A kind word to your class is very important.** The ageless teacher Solomon knew this when he wrote in Proverbs 12:25: *Heaviness in the heart of man makes it stoop:* **but a good word makes it glad.** There is a story of a young king by the name of Rehoboam who asked for advice about dealing with people. King Solomon's senior advisors gave him counsel which would serve you well also:

If you will be a servant to these people today, and serve them, and answer them, and ***speak good words to them****, then they will be your servants forever.* (1 Kings 12:7-16).

5. LESSON. (Philippians, for example)

✦ **SEED.** Define the topic. The apostle tells us right away why he is writing. In Philippians, Paul quickly states what is on his heart: **the need to remain steadfast in the Christian walk.** *God who began the good work within you will keep right on helping you <u>grow in his grace</u> until his task within you is finally finished.* (Philippians 1:6, TLB). This is the seed, or starting point, for the whole lesson. The good teacher will **define the goal and clarify the necessity of learning the topic** up front in order to motivate the class to learn. He then explains specifically what it means to grow in grace.
- *defending the truth* (Phil. 1:7, TLB)
- *telling others about Christ* (1:7, TLB)
- *overflow more and more with love for others, and at the same time keep on growing in spiritual knowledge and insight* (1:9, TLB)
- *to help you grow and become happy in your faith* (1:25, TLB)
- *standing side by side* (1:27, TLB)
- *receiving "the privilege not only of trusting him but also of suffering for him."* (1:29, TLB)

So, Paul defines the topic at the beginning. Now, if Paul had stopped here, by simply telling them to "stay the course," he would have not been much help. He also needed to encourage and exhort them.

✦ **NEED.** Why students need to learn this lesson. The good teacher will use scripture to lead his class through the advantages of learning and the consequences of ignorance.

- **Positive Motivation: The blessings and benefits of learning this lesson.**
  Paul tells the Philippians what **blessings** come from following his teaching:
    - Their conduct *"will bring much praise and glory to the Lord."* (1:11)
    - They need to emulate the Lord's attitude in order to receive **the rewards** of heaven. *"Your attitude should be the kind that was shown us by Jesus Christ, who, though he was God, did not demand and cling to his rights as God, but laid aside his mighty power and glory, taking the disguise of a slave and becoming like men.... Yet it was because of this that God raised him up to the heights of heaven."* (Philippians 2:5-9, TLB)
    - He reminds them of how glad he will be when the Lord returns to find the fruits of his ministry.
    - Finally, he promises to send his fellow ministers Timothy and Epaphroditus to help them.
- **Motivation through the consequences of ignoring the lesson.**
    - Paul knew that adults don't change until they can see that the pain of disobedience outweighs the effort of obedience. So he pointed out the consequences of not following his advice: that the Philippians' character would come under verbal attack. He stated that *"I want you always to see clearly the difference between right and wrong, and to be inwardly clean, **no one being able to criticize you** from now until our Lord returns."* (1:10, TLB)
    - In Chapter 2, Paul restated the consequence of lukewarm Christianity: *"In everything you do, stay away from complaining and arguing, so that **no one can speak a word of blame against you.**"* (2:14,15, TLB) Paul made sure that they knew their testimony would suffer if they failed to care for one another. When you are teaching, it is critical to point out **both** the blessings of obedience **and** the consequences of disobedience. Please remember that you are not simply passing on information: you are *persuading*. Make the decision clear and obvious. *"Patience can persuade a prince and soft speech breaks bones."* (Proverbs 25:15)

By now, the Philippians know **what** to do and **why** to do it. However, they do not know **how** to grow. So, Paul moves from general guidance to ***specific instructions***.

✦ **FEED.** The Scriptures on the topic. Earlier, Paul had given general directions to *"let your conduct be worthy of the gospel of Christ."* Now, he explains in detail what this means.

- **Loving one another**: *"having the same love."* (Phil. 2:2)
- **Displaying unity**: *"of one mind."* (Phil. 2:2)
- **Not arguing**: *"Let nothing be done through strife or vainglory."* (2:3)
- **Respecting one another highly**: *"in lowliness of mind let each esteem other better than themselves."* (2:3)
- **Protecting others' interests**: *"Look not every man on his own things, but every man also on the things of others."* (2:4)
- Moreover, Paul devotes Chapter 3 to **attitude**, telling them not to trust in their own traditions. Paul discounts his own credentials (circumcision and training as a Pharisee) and then states *"I count all things but loss for the excellency of the knowledge of Christ Jesus my Lord."* (Philippians 3:8) He then contrasts the Christian walk with that of the enemies of Christ, *"whose end is destruction, whose god is their belly, and whose glory is in their shame-who set their mind on earthly things."* (Philippians 3:19-20) Paul supported each of his points with facts and a contemporary (bad) example, to illustrate conduct to avoid.

- **DEED.** How to apply the lesson. In the final chapter, Paul reminds them to live out what he has taught in specific ways.

He asks that:
- Euodias and Syntyche make peace with one another. (4:2)
- The Philippians help these two Christians. (4:3)
- The Philippians always be full of joy in the Lord. (4:4)
- They not worry, but rather pray about everything. (4:6)
- They think about things that are "true and good and right." (4:8)
- They continue to support his ministry. (4:17)
- Paul continues to mention good outcomes and the rewards of following his teaching. He encouraged them to practice what they knew.

"Keep putting into practice all you learned from me and saw me doing, and the God of peace will be with you." (Philippians 4:9, TLB)

"What makes me happiest is the well-earned reward you will have because of your kindness." (Philippians 4:17, TLB)

6. Paul often closed with a blessing.

You may also choose to close in prayer. Paul's closing to the Philippians was: *"The blessings of our Lord Jesus Christ be upon your spirits."* (Philippians 4:23) Other blessings are found in Romans 15:33 and 16:24; 1 Corinthians 16:23; 2 Corinthians 13:14; and Ephesians 6:23 Here is a wonderful blessing that the Lord gave to Moses in Numbers 6:24-26 (NKJV):

The Lord bless you and keep you;
The Lord make His face shine upon you,
And be gracious to you;
The Lord lift up His countenance upon you,
and give you peace.

This would make an excellent closing.

Chapter 9

Preparing and Delivering the Lesson

Stir up the gift of God. (2 Timothy 1:6)

The Inspiration for the Subject

Pastor Milton Poole says, "God is in the *puttin'* business", because he puts desires into our hearts: *"what my **God had put in my heart** to do."* (Nehemiah 2:12) God will also place a desire in you to share your knowledge. Your nearly uncontrollable desire, or passion, will show through when you teach.

God chooses to reveal the things of his Kingdom to us. Deuteronomy 29:29 tells us, *"Those things which are revealed belong unto us and to our children for ever."* In Jeremiah 33:3, God commands us to ask him to reveal new truths to us: *"Call unto me, and I will answer you, and show you great and mighty things, which you know not."*

The subject matter is one part of God's blessing to your students. The other is his blessing on you: because the Lord has given you *"the tongue of the learned"* to *"know how to speak a word in season to him who is weary."* (Isaiah 50:4) God gives teachers timely topics.

Topical Lessons

Almost all Bible lessons are topical in some way. When Jesus told a parable, he was illustrating an idea, principle, or virtue; in other words, a topic. Even an entire chapter, or book of the Bible often contains a single dominant theme. If you teach the story of David and Goliath, the central theme of faith emerges. If you study Samson and Delilah, the subject of sin surfaces. Topical studies have the biggest impact on adults because they are concentrated. This single focus provides a more in-depth understanding of one subject. Students can remember one topic covered in depth more easily than a chronological lesson touching a number of different ideas.

Furthermore, the teacher will find the research for a topical study more enjoyable and manageable. Moreover, your research will transition **directly into a lesson plan** because the information is modular in nature. For the most part, lesson development is a matter of collecting and grouping scriptures under the various points they support.

Prepare your lesson with the presentation in mind. The lesson has four major sections:

1. **SEED:** Defining the topic biblically. The kernel of truth from which your lesson grows.

2. **NEED:** Clarifying the need for your students to learn and practice this teaching in their lives. (And pointing out the consequences of not learning this information)

3. **FEED:** Leading the class through a progressive examination of your topic, point by point.

4. **DEED:** Challenging your students to apply the lesson, explaining the steps required, and pointing out specific ways to put their knowledge into action.

There is a two-fold blessing in preparing and presenting the lesson.

The man who chops his own firewood is warmed twice.
— Henry Ford

Preparing and Delivering the Lesson

Part 1: SEED

Getting Their Attention

"And when the Lord saw that he turned aside to see, God called unto him." (Exodus 3:4)

Before you can teach anyone anything, you must get his attention. You can stir your students' interest by any of the following means:

- **Arouse their curiosity.** The teacher can throw out a few facts about the topic without revealing the subject. The students will begin to ponder the possible topics that fit these clues and they will begin to listen more carefully to your descriptors.
- **Ask them a question.** This puts the ball in the students' court. If there is no immediate answer, a nice pause is appropriate. This causes them to think of a possible response.
- **Tell them that the devil does not want them to know what you're about to teach.** This is always true, because the devil doesn't want any truth known. This also ascribes some mystique to the topic and conveys importance.
- **Tell them they will learn something that most people don't know.** This is a motivator and a self-esteem builder.
- **Tell them that you're going to cover some "really good stuff" today.** This is always true, because the Bible holds the best lessons for life.

Defining Your Topic

Unless you utter by the tongue words easy to understand, how will it be known what is spoken? (1 Corinthians 14:9)

In teaching on a topic, it is important to start with its biblical definition. This includes pointing out the difference between the Bible's definition and the world's perception. In other words, explain what the topic is, as well as what it is not. Oftentimes, contemporary definitions are culturally or situationally-based, such as with the term "submission." Some would define submission as a state of being dominated. However, the scriptural definition conveys following God-ordained authority joyfully. Likewise, the term "meek" is widely misunderstood. While the scriptural definition for meekness is controlled strength, some today would define it as acting fearfully.

Contrasting the true definition of your topic with the misconceptions held in modern life will open the eyes of your students and align them with biblical truth. The correct understanding of your topic lays the foundation on which subsequent modules are built.

Your job is to gather practical information and break it down into smaller, digestible elements. God told the prophet Habakkuk, *"Write my answer on a billboard,* **large and clear,** *so that anyone can read it at a glance."* (Habakkuk 2:2, TLB)

Part 2: NEED

Motivating Your Class

*But his delight is in the law of the Lord;
and in his law he meditates day and night.* (Psalm 1:2)

After your introduction, you want your class to follow your lesson plan. But in order for them to journey along with you, they must know that they are going somewhere worthwhile. King Solomon pointed out that people work for personal reasons, **to obtain something**. *"The person who labors, labors for himself."* (Proverbs 16:26 NKJV)

People, even Christians, need incentives. Create a desire to learn by showing them the rewards of learning the lesson. Tell them *why and how* this message will benefit them. Also, some students can be prodded into action by highlighting the hazards of *not* knowing the topic. George Washington once declared to his soldiers that he would shoot them with his own pistol if they ran in battle. That's strict motivation at its utmost, but entirely effective. If your students realize that they will suffer not knowing the material, they will be much more likely to embrace your teaching.

Proverbs 17:16 says that, unless people *want* to learn, all our efforts will be wasted. Attaching a reward to learning is biblical. A perfect example is found in Hebrews 10:36, *"For you have need of **patience**, that, after you have done the will of God, you might **receive the promise**."*

As you review the Bible, look for scriptures that tell:

✦ The blessings received from knowing and applying the lesson.

✦ The unpleasant consequences of *not* knowing and *not* applying the lesson.

Preparing and Delivering the Lesson

Part 3: FEED

*He shall feed his flock like a shepherd:
he shall gather the lambs with his arm, and carry them in his bosom,
and shall gently lead those that are with young.* (Isaiah 40:11)

Gathering Verses on Your Topic
Your word is a lamp unto my feet, and a light unto my path.
(Psalm 119:105)

Your goal is to present your topic so clearly that no one can get lost. *"Whoever walks the road, although a fool, shall not go astray."* (Isaiah 35:8) Ask God to illuminate his principles completely and to lead you in constructing the lesson. He has said: *"I will make darkness light."* (Isaiah 42:16) Also pray that God will anoint you to receive and teach all that He has for you.

Using your Bible and Concordance or your personal computer and Bible software, look for:

✦ Verses that provide all perspectives on your topic.
✦ Parables or Bible stories that illustrate your message points.

The Holy Spirit will bring scriptures to mind which you should find and record.
Using a Bible software program, you can search both the Old and New Testaments instantly to find verses which you can "cut and paste" into your lesson: ***very useful!*** For example, if you are teaching on forgiveness, several scriptures may come to mind, such as "he is faithful and just to forgive our sins" and "who forgives all your iniquities." Using your Bible software, you can find a verse by simply typing in one or two of the words in the verse.

As you gather and review the scriptures, you will notice that the scriptures support various aspects of your subject. For example, several scriptures support the fact that God's forgiveness is **unearned**. So, group together two or three scriptures under the heading, ***"Forgiveness is Unearned."*** Several other scriptures support the point that God **commands us** to forgive. Group two or three supporting scriptures under your second point, ***"God Commands Us to Forgive."*** In this way you can paint a clear picture of all aspects of forgiveness and justify each point with Bible verses. Two or three verses per point is enough: *"by the mouth of two or three witnesses every word may be established."* (Matthew 18:16)

Having gathered and grouped your Bible verses, you will see that some principles about your topic are foundational. In other words, they are the basis for the remainder of the teaching. For example, on the subject of forgiveness, Ephesians 4:32 commands us to forgive and tells us why we should forgive: *"And be kind one to another, tenderhearted, forgiving one another, even as God for Christ's sake have forgiven you."* Such a verse provides the fundamental reason for forgiveness: God's forgiveness of us. This starting point is like the roots of a tree that support upward growth and expansion.

Another wonderful feature of your Bible software is that it contains numerous Bible translations. Reading verses in several versions will give you a broader and deeper understanding of the meaning of the scripture.

In gathering information, remember the many wonderful source books that are available on a multitude of topics. Excellent Christian authors from conservative, mainline denominations have illuminated doctrines of the Christian faith and condensed enormous amounts of research for teachers. Christian schools and seminaries also offer a wide variety of on-line and correspondence courses. Furthermore, the internet contains many devotionals and essays written by Christian scholars.

Regardless of the sources you employ when researching your lesson topic, you will get an overall impression about the subject which you can boil down into a single statement. This statement, or central theme, will help you focus your presentation. In constructing your lesson, this central truth should be crystal clear in your mind and resident in your heart. **Clarity brings passion** and passion results in enthusiastic teaching.

Adults want to learn, but they don't always want to be taught. So you have the delicate task of sharing your well documented lesson without cramming it down their throats. You want to facilitate a fertile and pleasant learning environment wherein their hearts are open to God's truth and they can discover his principles themselves.

Whatever approach you choose, Scripture should be the central authority for your teaching. God has assured us that his word will be successful: ***"It shall not return to Me void, but it shall accomplish what I please, and it shall prosper in the thing for which I sent it."*** (Isaiah 55:11, NKJV) *"All Scripture is given by inspiration of God, and is profitable for doctrine, for reproof, for correction, for instruction in righteousness, that the man of God may be complete, thoroughly equipped for every good work."* (2 Timothy 3:16-17 NKJV) Please understand the power of Scripture. Jesus said, *"It is the Spirit who gives life; the flesh profits nothing. The words that I speak to you are spirit, and they are life."* (John 6:63)

In the King James version, Luke 1:37 reads "For with God nothing shall be impossible".

God's word has power: to create, to teach, to heal, to enlighten, to strengthen, to restore, to comfort.

Preparing and Delivering the Lesson

Illustrations.

In addition to the scriptural structure of your lesson, support your main points with illustrations. The best illustration is a story that demonstrates several points. For example, if you were teaching on sin, your points would include that sin blinds, betrays, binds, and belittles. So, your lesson might contain the following scriptures:

- *In whom the god of this world has **blinded** the minds of them which believe not.* (2 Corinthians 4:3-4)
- *And he would fain have filled his belly with the husks that the swine did eat: and **no man gave unto him**.* (Luke 15:16)
- *For of whom a man is overcome, of the same is he brought in **bondage**.* (2 Peter 2:19)
- *Poverty and **shame** shall be to him that refuses instruction.* (Proverbs 13:18)

Although there are several points you are making about sin, the story of **Samson** illustrates them all. This all-in-one illustration is easy to remember.

Techniques to Gain Class Participation During the "FEED" Segment

God gave them knowledge and skill in all learning and wisdom.
(Daniel 1:17)

- **Ask "anyone" to read a verse.** This is a superb way to gain participation without putting anyone on the spot. Of course, do not criticize the Bible translation used by your students. Compliment and thank them for reading.

- **Point out the specific truth that you want to emphasize from the verse read.**
  For example, if you are teaching about God's provision for each and every need we have, you could ask someone to read Philippians 4:19, *"But my God shall supply all your need according to his riches in glory by Christ Jesus."* You should draw attention to the word "all" because you are focusing on God's provision for every need, no matter how small or great. You are a teacher because you have an insight in the scriptures. You can spot and highlight specific impact words.
  i. You might ask, "Only our *big* needs?"
  ii. You also might ask what kinds of needs the verse is talking about.
  iii. Another technique is to playfully "misread" the verse: "But my God shall supply *most of* our needs according to his riches in glory…." This will reinforce what the verse really says as they catch the misreading.

- **Participate in the discussion yourself.** You are there to point out or illuminate the key truths in the verses. This is your gift, to see and interpret things that others overlook.

- **Encourage students to inject their thoughts, verses, and testimonials.** The great teacher King Solomon, understood and appreciated the value of others' input: *"As iron sharpens iron, so a man sharpens the countenance of his friend."* (Proverbs 27:17 NKJV) In addition to the knowledge that you impart, you are also providing a place for Christians to encourage and comfort one another. Bible class is more "heart surgery" than brain surgery.

- **Encourage questions.** Questions are wonderful opportunities to discover what your students are thinking. Questions also reveal that your students are comfortable with you and are paying attention. This is an honor to you and should not be viewed as a challenge to your knowledge or authority. There is no need to rebuff a question as being off the subject. Rather, comment that the student has brought up a "good question." This is the most receptive time you will ever have with the student: this is the "teachable moment" for which you have been praying. Don't embarrass them with an answer that discredits their question. If you do, you will appear uninterested in your students.

- **Use stories that illustrate your point. People remember stories.**
  To explain what happens when you receive Jesus Christ as Lord and Savior, Reverend Doug Page told the true story of someone who had been dying of cancer. A bone marrow donor came forward and skilled doctors performed a successful transplant. Not only had she been cured of her fatal disease, but she had acquired the same genetic design as the donor! This was the result of having received the donor's bone marrow cells, which produce DNA. This remarkable story illustrates how Christ's sacrifice makes us right with God. He gives us eternal life and replaces our sinful nature with his righteousness.
  What a memorable and powerful analogy!

- **Remember that the "Why" is critical to students.** People want to know the "why" behind the instructions. God is not opposed to this. For example, in Judges 3:1, God explains why he left small enemies for the younger generation to conquer: *"to test the new generation of Israel who had not experienced the wars of Canaan."*

- **Remember that the "How" is critical to students.** It is nothing less than cruel to admonish students to do something well without telling them **how** to do it. God gave explicit instructions for Noah's ark and specific instructions for Moses' tabernacle. Instructing in general terms is not very helpful when it comes time to apply a lesson. For example, simply telling someone to pray leaves a lot of room for interpretation. However, if you tell them what an attitude of prayer is, that God welcomes their prayers, and what hindrances to prayer exist, they have a much better footing. *Be specific.*

Preparing and Delivering the Lesson

Part 4: DEED *(The Criticality of Applying the Lesson)*

One verse applied is better than a thousand memorized.
Be doers of the word, and not hearers only. (James 1:22, NKJV)

Application: The Ultimate Goal
Moreover you shall provide out of all the people able men, such as fear God, men of truth. (Exodus 18:21)

Encourage them to apply the lesson and pray for the chance to exercise their newly acquired knowledge. You are trying to acquaint students with the Truth, who is a **Person**. Every lesson you will ever teach has to do with **becoming like Christ**, not just learning **about** him. This is why much of your Bible class involves ministering to your students through praise reports, prayer requests, and testimonies. You want them to **exercise what they learn**, and experience the Lord personally.

The Consequences of Not Applying the Lesson

Once God tells us to do something, he expects action. He wants us to perform in the manner prescribed. Your entire lesson is a waste of time if your students do apply what they learned. Furthermore, serious consequences follow disobedience.

King Saul lost his throne because of disobedience. He did not do everything God commanded in the way that God instructed.

*"Obedience is far better than sacrifice. He is much more interested in your listening to him than in your offering the fat of rams to him. For rebellion is as bad as the sin of witchcraft, and stubbornness is as bad as worshiping idols. And now **because you have rejected the word of Jehovah**, he has rejected you from being king."* (1 Samuel 15:22)

Another example of the consequences of disobedience is Achan. God cursed his own people because they did not follow his instructions.

"But there was sin among the Israelis. God's command to destroy everything except that which was reserved for the Lord's treasury was disobeyed. For Achan (the son of Carmi, grandson of Zabdi, and great-grandson of Zerah, of the tribe of Judah) took some loot for himself, and the Lord was very angry with the entire nation of Israel because of this." (Joshua 7:1, TLB)

But the Lord said to Joshua, *"Get up off your face!* **Israel has sinned and disobeyed** *my commandment and has taken loot when I said it was not to be taken; and they have not only taken it, they have lied about it and have hidden it among their belongings. That is why the people of Israel are being defeated. That is why your men are running from their enemies—for they are cursed. I will not stay with you any longer unless you completely rid yourselves of this sin."* (Joshua 7:10-11, TLB)

Specific Assignments
*For we are His workmanship, created in Christ Jesus **for good works**, which God prepared beforehand that we should walk in them.*

Point out how they can apply the lesson. Each Sunday, ask students for testimonials about how they applied what they learned the week before. If no one volunteers, tell them how you applied last week's lesson. Pray for opportunities to perform a good work in the coming week. God has prepared good works for us and *"long ages ago he planned that we should spend these lives in helping others."* (Ephesians 2:10, TLB) Without application, your class would be much like a baseball team that learns all the rules of the sport, but never plays a game. God has real life assignments for us to do. Psalms 111:10 tells us that *"growth in wisdom comes from **obeying** his laws."*

*Let your light so shine before men, that they may see your **good works**, and glorify your Father which is in heaven.* (Matthew 5:16)

The Nitty Gritty of Teaching Adult Sunday School

DEED
Application

FEED
Building Point #5
(Another aspect of topic)

FEED
Building Point #4
(Another aspect of topic)

FEED
Building Point #3
(Another aspect of topic)

FEED
Building Point #2
(Another aspect of topic)

FEED
BASIC Building Point #1
- Chief character of the topic
- Students should learn this point first.
- Other points rest upon this foundation.

Illustration (If possible, one "all-in-one" on the consequences of **not** applying the lesson).

NEED	**NEED**
CONSEQUENCE #1	**CONSEQUENCE #2**
(An undesirable result of **not** applying this lesson).	(An undesirable result of **not** applying this lesson).

Illustration (If possible, one "all-in-one" on the benefits of our topic).

NEED	**NEED**	**NEED**
BENEFIT #1	**BENEFIT #2**	**BENEFIT #3**
(A blessing from following this teaching)	*(A blessing from following this teaching)*	*(A blessing from following this teaching)*

SEED
FOUNDATION
(Biblical Definition or Principle)
NOTE: You can use an illustrative story, a bold statement, or a question to arouse interest in your topic.

Preparing and Delivering the Lesson

Sample Lesson Overview: WISDOM

I. **SEED:** The Biblical definition of Wisdom: "*Behold, the fear of the Lord, that is wisdom; and to depart from evil is understanding.* (Job 28:28) In other words, wisdom is **action**. The widely held notion is that wisdom is merely intellectual. "*Wisdom that comes down from above is first of all **pure** and full of quiet gentleness. Then it is peace-loving and courteous. It allows discussion and is willing to yield to others; it is full of **mercy** and good deeds. It is wholehearted and straightforward and **sincere**.*" (James 3:17,18 TLB)

II. **NEED:** (**Benefits** of Wisdom contrasted with the **Consequences** of Foolishness)
   (1) **Benefit:** Protection. "*When wisdom enters into your heart, and knowledge is pleasant unto your soul; Discretion shall preserve you, understanding shall keep you: To deliver you from the way of the evil man, from the man that speaks froward things.*" (Proverbs 2:10-12)
   (2) **Benefit:** Happiness. "*Happy is the man that finds wisdom, and the man that gets understanding.*" (Proverbs 3:13)
   (3) **Benefit:** Life, Grace, Safety. "*Keep sound wisdom and discretion: So shall they be life unto your soul, and grace to your neck. Then shall you walk in your way safely, and your foot shall not stumble.*" (Proverbs 3:21-22)
   (4) **Benefit:** Promotion, Honor. "*Exalt her, and she shall promote you: she shall bring you to honor, when you embrace her.*" (Proverbs 4:8)
   (5) **Benefit:** Judgment. "*By me kings reign, and princes decree justice. By me princes rule, and nobles, even all the judges of the earth.*" (Proverbs 8:15-16)
   (6) **Benefit:** Recognition. "*A man shall be commended according to his wisdom.*" (Proverbs 12:8)
   (7) **Benefit:** Insight. "*Wisdom is of more value than foolishness, just as light is better than darkness; for the wise man sees, while the fool is blind.*" (Ecclesiastes 2:13)
   (8) **Consequence of foolishness:** Alienation from God. "*The foolish shall not stand in your sight.*" (Psalms 5:5)
   (9) **Consequence of foolishness:** Ignorance. "*A foolish woman is clamorous: she is simple, and knows nothing.*" (Psalms 9:13)

III. **FEED:** All the features of the topic (wisdom), starting with the basic truth upon which the others are built.
   (1) **Foundational Point #1:** Understanding God's sovereignty is our starting point.
       a. "*The fear of the Lord is the beginning of wisdom: a good understanding have all they that do his commandments: his praise endures forever.*" (Psalms 111:10)
       b. "*The fear of the Lord is the instruction of wisdom; and before honor is humility.*" (Proverbs 15:33)
   (2) **Where can we find wisdom?**
       a. "*For **the Lord** gives wisdom.*" (Proverbs 2:6)
       b. "*When pride comes, then comes shame: but **with the lowly is wisdom**.*" (Proverbs 11:2)
       c. "*Only by pride comes contention: but **with the well advised is wisdom**.*" (Proverbs 13:10)
       d. "*If any of you lack wisdom, **let him ask** of God, that gives to all men liberally, and upbraids not; and it shall be given him.*" (James 1:5)
   (3) **Wisdom is the main thing.**
       a. *Wisdom is the **principal** thing; therefore get wisdom: and with all your getting get understanding.*" (Proverbs 4:7)
       b. "***How much better is it to get wisdom than gold!*** " (Proverbs 16:16)
       c. "*Wisdom is the main pursuit of sensible men.*" (Proverbs 17:24, TLB)
   (4) **Wisdom invites you to be wise.**
       a. "*Does not wisdom cry? And understanding put forth her voice? She stands in the top of high places, by the way in the places of the paths. She cries at the gates, at the entry of the city, at the coming in at the doors. Unto you, O men, I call; and my voice is to the sons of man.*" (Proverbs 8:1-4)
       b. "*I love all who love me. Those who search for me shall surely find me.* " (Proverbs 8:17)
   (5) **The wise are profitable, but the foolish are punished and die.**
       a. In the lips of him *that has understanding wisdom is found: but **a rod is for the back of him that is void of understanding.**"* (Proverbs 10:13)
       b. "*The lips of the righteous feed many: but **fools die for want of wisdom**.*" (Proverbs 10:21)

Interject a story, <u>either biblical or contemporary</u>, contrasting wise and foolish behavior.

Example: The parable from Matthew 7:24-27: "*Therefore whosoever hears these sayings of mine, and does them, I will liken him unto a wise man, which built his house upon a rock: And the rain descended, and the floods came, and the winds blew, and beat upon that house; and it fell not: for it was founded upon a rock. And every one that hears these sayings of mine, and does them not, shall be likened unto a **foolish man**, which built his house upon the sand: And the rain descended, and the floods came, and the winds blew, and beat upon that house; and it fell: and great was the fall of it.*"

IV. **DEED:** (Apply ourselves to wisdom): How long do you have to live wisely?
   a. We should make King David's prayer our own: "*So teach us to number our days, **that we may apply** our hearts unto wisdom.*" (Psalms 90:12) How many years do you have left?
   b. We should also adopt David's attitude toward God: "*As the hart pants after the water brooks, so pants my soul after you, O God.* "(Ps 42:1)
   c. Our wisdom should be clearly seen in our lives. "*If you are wise, live a life of steady goodness, so that only good deeds will pour forth. And if you don't brag about them, them you will be truly wise!*" (James 3:13b TLB)

Chapter 10

Butterflies, Nerves, and Palpitations

"Be of good courage, and he shall strengthen your heart." (your emotions) (Psalm 27:14)

Should you experience "butterflies" as you begin to speak, accept them as a kind reminder that you need God's help to teach. If the Sunday School class is successful, it won't be because of you, it will be because of God. So, don't assume complete responsibility for the outcome of the class: that burden is God's. Enjoy being a coworker with God.

In Isaiah, God reminds us that he is responsible for our success: *"I, even I, am he who comforts you and gives you all this joy. **So what right have you to fear mere mortal men**, who wither like the grass and disappear?"* (Isaiah 51:12, The Living Bible) It is not our place to assume God's sovereign role.

There is no need to fear your audience. *"Men are nothing but a mere breath; human beings are unreliable. When they are weighed in the scales, all of them together are lighter than air."* (Psalm 62:9)

When we approach the platform to teach, we should be **confident**, but not arrogant. We need to be assured that we are *"fearfully and wonderfully made,"* yet know that "without me (Jesus) you can do nothing." We should "stir up" the gift of teaching. *"For God has not given us the spirit of fear; but of power, and of love, and of a sound mind."* (2 Timothy 1:6-7) Teaching should be your greatest joy. The "real you" should emerge in the classroom.

If there is fear *prior* to speaking, recognize that this is only a fear of the future since the event has not yet occurred. Just deal with the step that you are taking at the moment (waiting to speak) and leave the future to God.

Professional athletes, such as L. James, know that emotions should be "not too high; not too low." This applies to teaching, also.

Should you experience a sudden, unexplained panic, it could be agoraphobia, which is a fear of being in public view. God delivers from agoraphobia, whether emotional or demonic. You have authority over evil spirits. Exercise it in the name of Jesus.

One thing that you should do several days before your class is to "pray through" for success. Pray for God to take responsibility for your class. Simply pray, and keep praying, until you feel God's anointing and know in your heart that God has blessed the upcoming lesson. *"One day Jesus told his disciples … that they must keep praying until the answer comes."* (Luke 18:1, TLB) Also, ask the Lord for a spirit of joy as you teach. You teach so much better when you're smiling.

· ·

Fulfilled

**This work is neither burden nor strife.
But a pleasant way to spend my life.**

**My face reflects the glow inside
True satisfaction I cannot hide**

**'Tis my soul that's smiling through
It's clear to see, *I love what I do*.**

· ·

The Lord is with thee, thou mighty man of valor. (Judges 6:12)

Being prepared is a great feeling!

Chapter 11

Useful In-Class Comments

"The Lord God has given me the tongue of the learned, that I should know how to speak a word in season to him that is weary."
(Isaiah 50:4)

- **Greetings / Blessing / Compliment**
  - I'm so pleased to see you all here on time.
  - You look good this morning.
  - Does anyone have guests you would like to introduce?
  - God bless you for your faithfulness in coming each Sunday.
- **Praise Reports**
  - Has the Lord done anything for you this week that you would like to tell us about?
  - Can anyone here tell the class how you applied our lesson from last Sunday?
- **Prayer Requests**
  - Are there any prayer requests? Spoken or unspoken?
  - Will anyone be traveling this week?
  - Shall we remember those in the news this week?
- **LESSON (SEED)** *To get their attention right away.*
  - We will be looking at something that the Lord talked about often.
  - We will be looking at a quality the Lord demonstrated often, but the apostles had a hard time .... with.
  - We'll be talking about something that God commanded us to do **every day**.
- **LESSON (NEED)** *To motivate them to learn.*
  - Why should we take time to learn about this topic?
  - What are the dangers of not knowing this information?
- **LESSON (FEED)** *Make sure the class gets the main point of your lesson.*
  - What does the sequence of events reveal about God's hand in the final resolution.
  - Why did God allow this story to unfold in this way?
  - Does anyone have any closing comments or questions? (Students will have important insight ... and probing questions).
  - The key to this matter is …
  - The larger issue is …
  - The secret of this is …
- **LESSON (DEED)** *Challenge them to take action.*
  - **Remember James 1:22:** *But be you **doers** of the word, and not hearers only.*
  - **The blessing is in the doing:** James 1:25. *But whoso looks into the perfect law of liberty, and . continues therein, he being not a forgetful hearer, but a doer of the work,* <u>**this man shall be blessed in his deed**</u>.
  - All our time here this morning will be wasted if you don't apply this lesson in the coming week. *One Bible verse followed is worth a thousand memorized.*
- **CLOSING PRAYER**
  - Lord, give us opportunities to apply what we have learned today.
  - Lord, give us wisdom to serve you in this area with willing hearts.
- **FAREWELL and BLESSING**
  - You all had some very good comments today. Thank you for your input.
  - God bless you and keep you until we see you again Sunday.
  - Don't forget to pray for me as I prepare our lesson for next week.

Chapter 12

Preparation Checklist

*"And your feet shod with the **preparation** of the gospel of peace."* (Ephesians 6:15)

Practice does *not* make perfect. *Perfect* practice makes perfect.

1. **MONDAY.**
   a. Have you begun to **pray well ahead of time**? Little prayer, little power. Great prayer, Great power. *"For the kingdom of God is not in word, but in power."* (1 Corinthians 4:20)
   b. *"Are you focused on doing your best? And if you don't do your best for him, he will pay you in a way that you won't like."* (Col . 3:25,TLB)
   c. **John Wesley said that God does nothing, except by prayer.** *"If any of you lack wisdom, let him ask of God, that gives to all men liberally, and upbraids not; and it shall be given him. "* (James 1:5) ***PRAY THROUGH*** for God's anointing.
   d. Pray for God to send students who need to hear this lesson.

2. **TUESDAY.**
   a. Begin preparing early enough to avoid being rushed. *"It is dangerous and sinful to rush into the unknown."* (Proverbs 19:2)
   b. *Study* the background and the context of your key passages. Read the verses in several Bible versions. *"Study to show yourself approved unto God, a workman that needs not to be ashamed, rightly dividing the word of truth."* (2 Timothy 2:15)

3. **WEDNESDAY.** Read the commentaries on the passage and ask what the biblical writer was expressing at the time he wrote it. The intent of the message is still valid today.

4. **THURSDAY.** Using Greek and Hebrew dictionaries, look up the definitions of words in their original languages. This gives a broader and deeper understanding of the meaning of the words.

5. **FRIDAY.**
   a. Review the scriptures in the lesson. *"Wherefore I will not be negligent to **put you always in remembrance of these things**, though you know them, and are established in the present truth."* (2 Peter 1:12)
   b. Do everything you know to do to prepare. *"Leave **nothing** undone that you ought to do."* (2 Timothy 4:5, TLB)
   c. Do your best to prepare. *"So, **as much as in me is**, I am ready to preach the gospel to you."* (Romans 1:15)
   d. Teach the lesson in the mirror.

6. **SATURDAY (Enjoy feeling prepared).**
   a. Take time to rest. Sometimes, the most spiritual thing you can do is rest.
   b. Pack your car on Saturday evening so you don't forget handouts or other visual aids.
   c. Have you prepared the classroom? *"He will take you to a large room all set up. Prepare …."* (Mark 14:15, TLB)
   d. Confidently expect God to do great things in your lesson. *"Let Israel hope (confidently, unchangingly, expect) in the Lord from henceforth and for ever."* (Psalm 131:3)

7. **SUNDAY.**
   a. **Verbally restrict the devil from the church building and grounds.** *Or else how can one enter into a strong man's house, and spoil his goods, except he first bind the strong man? and then he will spoil his house.* (Matthew 12:29)
   b. **Be confident, but not arrogant.**

i. *"Wherefore take unto you the whole armor of God, that you may be able to withstand in the evil day, and having done all, to stand."* (Ephesians 6:13)
ii. *"**Stir up the gift of God,** which is in you by the putting on of my hands. For God has not given us the spirit of fear; but of power, and of love, and of a sound mind."* (2 Tim 1:6-7)

c. **Be prepared to respond in a respectful way if someone challenges your teaching.** *"Quietly trust yourself to Christ your Lord and if anybody asks why you believe as you do, be ready to tell him, and do it **in a gentle and respectful way**.*" (1 Peter 3:15, TLB)

d. **Expect to learn something about attitude from your students.** *"These were more noble than those in Thessalonica, in that they received the word with all readiness of mind, and searched the scriptures daily, whether those things were so."* (Acts 17:11)

e. **Set the example.** *"Feed the flock of God; care for it **willingly**, not grudgingly; not for what you will get out of it, but because you are eager to serve the Lord. Don't be tyrants, but lead them by your good **example**, and when the Head Shepherd comes, your reward will be a never-ending share in his glory and honor."* (1 Peter 5:2-4)

f. **Be a friend to your students by sharing your personality with them.** *"So being affectionately desirous of you, we were willing to have imparted unto you, not the gospel of God only, but also **our own souls**, because you were dear unto us."*
(1 Thessalonians 2:8)

g. **Pray over each chair in the classroom.** Ask for God to open the mind and heart of each attendee to receive the message.

h. **Just before entering the classroom, declare:**
   i. *"I am made in the image of God."* (Genesis 1:27)
   ii. *"I am more than a conqueror through him that loved us."* (Romans 8:37)
   iii. *"I am fearfully and wonderfully made: a marvelous work and I know it deep down inside."* (Ps 139:14)

i. **Stop tweaking your lesson, relax and teach.** *"Go in this your might…have not I sent you?"* (Judges 6:14)

Chapter 13

The Best Thing a Student Can Give a Teacher: a Question

"Ask me of things ..." (Isaiah 45:11)

When a student asks a question, never view it as a challenge to your authority or knowledge. Rather, accept each question as the honor and the opportunity that it is.

When a student asks a question, it means the student:

- is paying attention.
- is motivated.
- believes the teacher knows the answer.
- believes the teacher will help him.
- trusts the teacher enough to become vulnerable.
- is in a "teachable moment."
- is showing respect to the teacher.

It also means that the teacher has an opportunity to:

- inform more fully.
- compliment the student.
- learn what is on the student's mind.
- follow the Lord's leading in giving the answer.
- start a class discussion.

We know that the apostles commended the Christians in Berea because they did not blindly accept everything the apostles said. Rather, they verified that scripture confirmed the apostles' teaching.

Acts 17:11

*"These were more noble than those in Thessalonica, in that they received the word with all readiness of mind, and **searched the scriptures daily, whether those things were so.**"* You don't want students who never question anything, nodding politely and taking notes. You want students who examine, question, and analyze.

In the Hebrew, the word lāmäd is used in the Bible for **both** teacher and student. This means that the student is interwoven in the teaching process and discovers information for himself. Likewise, the teacher is responsible for continuing to learn.

Students account for much of the fun that teachers have and teachers account for much of the enjoyment that students experience.

The Precious Moment

I had wondered how my words were received
Now all my qualms have been relieved
I know their curiosity has been fanned.
By this thoughtful look and raised hand.
A great compliment has been sent.
A celestial sparkle: a teachable moment!
This is my chance to touch heart and mind
Just the right words I must find.
The student has opened his soul to me.
Lord, send your Truth, light and free.
Yes, guide this faithful saint so dear
Skillfully down your path so near.
This moment is wonderful, delightful in time.
A simple question, how truly sublime!

Chapter 14

The Best Thing a Teacher Can Give a Student: A Compliment

When Jesus heard it, he marvelled, and said to them that followed, Verily I say unto you, I have not found so great faith, no, not in Israel. (Matthew 8:10)

Jesus told her, *"**your faith is large**, and your request is granted."* (Matthew 15:28, TLB)

Do you know why you still have your high school yearbook? It's because of all the kind words your friends, teachers, and coaches wrote inside. Words are powerful ways to encourage, inspire, and express affection. A student will treasure your compliment until the day he dies. Use the privilege and honor of your position well. Build their esteem and confidence. **Make someone's day!**

Anxious hearts are very heavy but a word of encouragement does wonders!
(Proverbs 12:25, TLB)

....

Years ago, at a high school graduation ceremony, the valedictorian came to the microphone to deliver his commencement speech. To the amazement of his classmates, he told the heart wrenching story of how hard it had been for him as a new student at the school. Without any friends, he had been ridiculed and mocked so cruelly by the other students that he had decided to kill himself. While walking home that day, he stumbled, spilling his books all over the sidewalk. To his surprise, another student came over, helped him and began a friendly conversation with him. This brief encounter changed his attitude and was the first step toward a happy and rewarding social life.

Never, ever, underestimate the mighty power of your kind and encouraging words. Indeed,

"Death and life are in the power of the tongue." (Proverbs 18:21)

Kind words are like honey— sweet to the soul and healthy for the body. (Proverbs 16:24, NLT)

If you will be kind to these people and please them by speaking kind words to them, they will be your servants forever. (2 Chronicles 10:7, Holcomb Christian Standard Bible)

....

The fact that students make mistakes is no reason to dampen their enthusiasm. Have you ever been a few minutes late? Ever day dreamed in class? But your teacher, someone respected by the whole class, did not embarrass you in front of everyone. You and your class are all members of the same family: and you never want to offend your family. If Jesus had kept a record of all the things his apostles did wrong, there wouldn't be a church today. Handle their mistakes like Jesus did: look past who they are to see **who they will become**. Keep on teaching. The word of God that you plant in the hearts of your students will eventually produce much fruit.

So shall my word be that goes forth out of my mouth: it shall not return unto me void, but it shall accomplish that which I please, and it shall prosper in the thing whereto I sent it.
(Isaiah 55:11)

My best friend is the one who brings out the best in me. — Henry Ford

Chapter 15

A Word About Attendance

"Because strait is the gate, and narrow is the way, which leads unto life, and few there be that find it." (Matthew 7:14)

Noah was a preacher of righteousness, yet he never won a single convert other than his own family members. The Lord told Ezekiel that *"the house of Israel will not hearken unto thee; for they will not hearken unto me."* (Ezekiel 3:7) And in John Chapter 3, we see that even Jesus experienced a drop in attendance: "From that time many of his disciples went back, and walked no more with him." (By the way, the departure of some students can be a good thing).

Low attendance does not indicate poor teaching: nor does high attendance always reflect excellent teaching. In fact, strong teaching and intense prayer will cause some to leave. Consider that the Gergesenes asked Jesus to leave after he cast demons out of two men. *"And, behold, the whole city came out to meet Jesus: and when they saw him, they besought him that he would depart out of their coasts."* (Matthew 8:34) This was **too much** of God's Kingdom for them.

While you are responsible to do your best in teaching, you are not responsible for the number of people who attend your class. Sometimes, the Lord taught only Peter, James, and John. Many times he spoke only to the twelve. Your task is not to tailor the message to attract large numbers. Your job is to teach the truth, recognizing that some may not receive what you say. Nevertheless, Jesus tells you *"He who receives you receives Me, and he who receives Me receives Him who sent Me."* (Matthew 10:40)

But use your judgment in the level of intensity you show. There is such a thing as "preaching people out of church."

Often, a small group is the best place to teach and exhort those who have delicate matters on their hearts. A small class allows for intimate sharing and personal questions that might not arise in a larger setting. Pray that the Lord will send those who need to hear your lesson and those who will contribute to the class. Ask God to divert anyone who would detract from the lesson.

God may allow you to present the Bible to those who reject the truth

One possible reason for this is Judgment Day. God will have evidence of the opportunities and instruction he offered, so that they are "without excuse." (Romans 1:20)

Factors that Help Attendance

✦ Your pastor's support is critical. If he will do these things, it will show students that Sunday School is a high priority:
  - Regularly remind the congregation about the class topics and what time class begins.
  - Encourage people to attend.
  - Drop by class occasionally.

✦ It is important to let the class out in time for fellowshipping, a break, and finding a seat in church.

✦ The support of a few key class members is important.
  - Capitalize on their ability to influence others.
  - Gain their support

A Word About Attendance

✦ Home Bible study groups may affect class attendance substantially. If your church has home Bible study groups, the members of these groups often attend the same Sunday School class together. This is especially true when the home group and the class are organized by age group.

✦ Remembering birthdays creates loyalty, as do other personal acts of kindness, such as a phone call now and then or a "get well" card. The route to the mind goes through the heart.

✦ Class participation creates happiness. Students enjoy contributing their opinions and hearing those of others. Ask questions periodically during the lesson and kindle a lively discussion.

✦ On a practical note, some value handouts because it makes it easy to follow the lesson.

✦ There is an old saying that has some truth for teachers: Catch on fire for the Lord and people will come to see you burn.

Chapter 16

Why Stories Work

"His usual method of teaching was to tell the people stories."
(Mark 4:2, The Living Bible)

Stories are pleasant. They entertain without requiring anything from us. You remember your childhood years, when at bedtime you nestled into your pillow, and asked your parents for something special to end the fun-packed day. ***"Please tell me a story."*** We grew up listening to stories as we rested cozily under warm covers. Those stories were the last words you heard as you drifted off to sleep.

Likewise, your elementary school teachers read time honored stories to a class full of attentive students, thankful for a break from their studies. Your Sunday School teachers also shared the sagas of David and Goliath, Noah and the Ark, and Daniel in the Lion's Den. As we have grown up, stories have entertained us, taught us, and united us in our shared beliefs and culture. It is no wonder we all love stories.

Stories are to Christian education what sports are to physical education. When you play softball or basketball, you don't think about the running or jumping involved because your mind is on the game. The physical conditioning is painless and fun and at the end of the game, you have had a great workout. Likewise, a story takes your students on a vacation away from the confines of your classroom. While they follow the adventures, triumphs and narrow escapes of the characters, they are learning biblical truths. Yet, how much more enjoyable than a lecture!

Stories are also wonderful launching pads for class discussions. For example, you could ask students how they would feel if they were in Daniel's shoes. If discussing disobedience, and Jonah's time in the fish's belly, you could ask what "holding tank" God might use today to deal with a rebellious Christian. When talking about Shadrach, Meshach, and Abednego, you could ask if anyone ever felt like they were also surrounded by a heathen culture.

In short, there are plenty of stories in the Bible that illustrate your point. Don't worry about your adult students being too familiar with the Bible stories. **You will notice a heightened interest when you interject stories into your lesson** and you will be able to emphasize God's hand throughout the events. Whether from the Bible or your own experiences, bless your students with a story. And when you tell it, don't forget to relive the adventure yourself! Be expressive and animated.

A Word About Story Telling

Stories are the secret weapon of teachers. A story entertains while teaching a central truth. The Bible is full of colorful stories which Christians and unbelievers remember easily; such as The Good Samaritan and The Prodigal Son. All of these have some things in common:

✦ **Heroes and unlikely endings (by natural standards).** Though from a lowly regarded race, the good Samaritan exceeded the Jewish priests in nobility. Though wasteful and broken, the repentant "prodigal son" received the best robe while his long laboring brother received an attitude adjustment. *"For my thoughts are not your thoughts, neither are your ways my ways, says the Lord."* (Isaiah 55:8) Due to God's mercy, there are many unlikely endings in the Bible and in our own lives. Jesus came *"to give sight to those who are spiritually blind and to show those who think they see that they are blind."* (John 9:39, TLB)

✦ **Drama.** Something hangs in the balance in each Bible story or parable. The life of the traveler depended on the compassion of the good Samaritan. The well-being of the prodigal son was contingent on the mercy of his father.

✦ **Comparison and Contrast**. The good Samaritan was a despised minority while the priests who passed by were ever so dignified and honored. The prodigal son was impetuous and frivolous while his brother was dutiful and hardworking. Jesus often used vivid contrast.

1. When he observed the poor widow donate only **"two mites,"** Jesus pointed out she had given more than all the rich combined because she had put in **"all that she had."** (Mark 12:41-44) In contrasting the two, Jesus exposed the true poverty of the wealthy.

2. When the Lord visited the Pharisee for dinner, a sinful woman washed his feet with tears, wiped them with her hair, kissed his feet, and anointed them with expensive ointment. When the Pharisee's thoughts turned to judgment, Jesus reminded his host that he had not shown any of the honor which this outcast woman had: he had not provided water for his feet, neither a kiss, nor oil for his head. (Luke 7: 37-46) In comparing the receptions of these two, Jesus revealed that repentance receives forgiveness, but self-righteousness receives judgment.

✦ **Jesus used everyday language.** Jesus spoke in understandable and contemporary terms. He used words from the working world. Additionally, both Jesus and Paul spoke on the level of their students. Note that Jesus' stories concerned **tangible items**. He spoke about a pearl of great price and about a lost coin. Such real objects stick in the minds of listeners and reminded them of the truth of the story. *"For the kingdom of God is not in word, but in power."* (1 Corinthians 4:20)

✦ **Jesus taught only what his disciples could take in at the time.** Use good judgment in choosing subject matter, because not all people are on the same spiritual level. You would not teach calculus to an elementary student, and you should not teach over anyone's head. Jesus said *"I still have many things to say to you, but you cannot bear them now."* (John 16:12 NKJV) Paul, in 1 Corinthians 2:6, stated, *"we speak wisdom among those who are mature."* The spiritual level of your students determines how much you can teach. Taken to the extreme, we are cautioned not to put spiritual treasures before those who have no appreciation for them. *"Give not that which is holy unto the dogs, neither cast ye your pearls before swine, lest they trample them under their feet, and turn again and rend you."* (Matthew 7:6) Use good judgment in what you teach. The lesson should be appropriate to their spiritual temperature and knowledge.

✦ **Jesus was human, not haughty.** A little humor is disarming and warms up the class. Good-hearted laughter is something everyone can share. Just make sure you don't embarrass anyone. Jesus himself was not too formal to poke a little fun at the religious peacocks of his day. On one occasion, he said, *"You would think these Jewish leaders and these Pharisees were Moses, the way they keep making up so many laws!"* (Matthew 23:1-2, The Living Bible)

Chapter 17

Jesus' Favorite Teaching Technique: *Contrast*

"Wisdom excels folly, as light excels darkness."
(Ecclesiastes 2:13, NKJV)

When telling a story, Jesus used a simple technique with powerful results: ***contrast.*** By comparing a good example with a bad example, the Lord imparted an appreciation of the enormous gulf between obedience and disobedience, righteousness and unrighteousness, wisdom and foolishness.

This Jewish tradition is also seen in the book of Proverbs, written by the wisest man alive at the time, Solomon. The following proverbs clearly illustrate the use of contrast.

- *"The fear of the Lord is the beginning of knowledge: but fools despise wisdom and instruction."* (Proverbs 1:7)

- *"A soft answer turns away wrath, but harsh words cause quarrels."* (Proverbs 15:1, TLB)

- *"For you turned away from me – to death; your own complacency will kill you. Fools! But all who listen to me shall live in peace and safety, unafraid."* (Proverbs 1:32,33, TLB)

God's truths are predisposed to graphically contrast the ways of the world. In Genesis, Cain's offering and heart were not acceptable to God while his brother Abel gave his best in sincerity. In 1 Samuel, Goliath was self-reliant, while David was dependent on God. In Luke 10, Martha was busy waiting on her house guests, but Mary focused only on the Lord.

Jesus consistently contrasted good and bad qualities in his parables.

- In Luke 16, the Lord described a beggar *"full of sores,"* and a rich man who *"fared sumptuously every day."*

- In Matthew 7, he talked about *"a wise man, which built his house upon a rock"* and *"a foolish man, which built his house upon the sand."*

You can use Bible stories or modern day events to employ this technique. You can note the experiences of people in the news and compare sound and sinful conduct. Point out good models whom God rewards and those who forget God and suffer the consequences. Discuss the leaders, athletes, and other personalities of our time who are living for God despite the world around them. By doing so, you reinforce your points in everyday, contemporary terms. They will value self-control much more if they can see the ruin and shame of drunkenness. They will cherish heaven much more when they know about the torment, anguish, and fire of hell.

Since the devil offers alternatives to God's best, contrast these counterfeits with genuine truth. Later, when your students weigh the pain of sin against the blessings of obedience, they will make the right choice.

Chapter 18

A Picture is Worth a Thousand Words

Make it plain. (Habakkuk 2:2)

My ears had heard of you but now my eyes have seen you. (Job 42:5, NIV)

When your lesson covers a great deal of information, such as the kings of Israel, the judges of Israel, or the Lord's miracles, it is very helpful to provide your class with an overview. "Boiling down" the material helps your students to see the big picture, pick out recurring themes and keep events in order. For example, when discussing a long sequence of events, a simple time line is a wonderful visual aid.

You can create such charts yourself, or you can purchase them at your local Christian book store. Rose Publishing, of Torrance, California is a wonderful source of Biblical charts, graphs, and pictures. This graphic summarizes the cycle of sin, hardship, repentance, and redemption during the time of the Judges.

TROUBLE	PEOPLE PRAY TO GOD	GOD SENDS LEADER	PEACE	LEADER DIES	PEOPLE RETURN TO SIN
Conquest of the Promised Land.		the Lord spoke unto Joshua … (Joshua 1:1)	And the people served the Lord all the days of Joshua, and all the days of the elders that outlived Joshua, who had seen all the great works of the Lord, that he did for Israel. (Judges 2:7)	And Joshua the son of Nun, the servant of the Lord, died. (Judges 2:8)	And they forsook the Lord God. (Judges 2:12)
King of Mesopotamia dominates Israel 8 years. Therefore the anger of the Lord was hot against Israel, and he sold them … (Judges 3:8)	And when the children of Israel cried unto the Lord. (Judges 3:9)	The Lord raised up a deliverer, who delivered them… (Judges 3:9,10)	And the land had rest forty years. (Judges 3:11)	And Othniel the son of Kenaz died. (Judges 3:11)	And the children of Israel did evil again in the sight of the Lord. (Judges 3:12)
King of Moab dominates 18 years. … and the Lord strengthened Eglon the king of Moab against Israel … (Judges 3:12, 14)	But when the children of Israel cried unto the Lord, the Lord raised them up a deliverer. (Judges 3:15)	Ehud the son of Gera, a Benjamite, a man lefthanded … (Judges 3:15)	So Moab was subdued that day under the hand of Israel. And the land had rest fourscore years. (Judges 3:30)	Ehud was dead. (Judges 4:1)	And the children of Israel again did evil in the sight of the Lord, when Ehud was dead. (Judges 4:1)
King of Canaan dominates for 20 years. And the Lord sold them into the hand of Jabin king of Canaan … (Judges 4:2)	And the children of Israel cried unto the Lord (Judges 4:3)	And Deborah, a prophetess, the wife of Lapidoth, she judged Israel at that time. (Judges 4:4)	And the hand of the children of Israel prospered, and prevailed against Jabin the king of Canaan … (Judges 5:31) … and the land had rest forty years.	(Deborah is not mentioned in Scripture afterwards).	And the children of Israel did evil in the sight of the Lord… (Judges 6:1)
Midianites dominate 7 years. … and the Lord delivered them into the hand of Midian seven years. (Judges 6:1)	And it came to pass, when the children of Israel cried unto the Lord because of the Midianites … (Judges 6:7)	And the angel of the Lord appeared unto him (Gideon), and said unto him, the Lord is with thee, thou mighty man of valor. (Judges 6:12)	Thus was Midian subdued before the children of Israel, so that they lifted up their head no more. And the country was in quietness forty years in the days of Gideon. (Judges 8:28)	And Gideon the son of Joash died in a good old age, and was buried … (Judges 8:32)	And it came to pass, as soon as Gideon was dead, that the children of Israel turned again, and went a whoring …. (Judges 8:33)

Chapter 19

30 Ways to Mess Up Your Class

"Dead flies will cause even a bottle of perfume to stink! Yes, a small mistake can outweigh much wisdom and honor."
(Ecclesiastes 10:1, TLB)

Many teachers practice techniques which hinder their teaching. Avoid these mistakes:

1. Not asking God to anoint you.
Always take time to pray for God's anointing. We all need a touch from heaven.

2. Not preparing.
Research beyond the material you plan to teach. It will serve you well.

3. Writing everything you say on a board or a flip chart as you teach.
When you write each point on a board, it slows your presentation considerably. It is much better to prepare your points ahead of time. You can create training aids using:
 a. Computer-generated slides.
 b. Pre-written flip charts or white boards (Hand-written charts have a personal touch).
 c. Individual hand-outs.

4. Using an unpleasant tone of voice.
"Kind words are like honey-enjoyable and healthful." (Proverbs 16:24, The Living Bible)
There is no need to bark out lectures. Use a pleasant, enthusiastic, and friendly tone of voice.

5. Criticizing a Bible translation.
Some students enjoy The Living Bible and some enjoy the King James. We should be thankful they have a favorite translation.

6. Breaking eye contact.
If you have ever had a teacher who paused and took his glasses off to read, you have felt the **loss of energy** in the classroom. Maintain eye contact whenever possible. If you don't have eye contact, you don't have communication.

7. Failing to gain class participation.
Get the "audience" involved. It's the secret of every popular television game show. There are three requirements for a happy class: class participation, class participation, class participation.

8. Not telling them *WHY* the lesson is important.
In the back of every student's mind is one question about your lesson: "So what?" Turn this around by asking the class, "What does this mean to you? Why should you focus on what we have talked about?" If they don't formulate a good answer, provide an explanation.

9. Not telling them *HOW* to apply the lesson.
Informing your class that they need to do something does not enable them to do it. You must tell them what steps to take. Simply directing them to "fast" or to "evangelize" does not enable them to do either. Be specific in your guidance, assuming they know nothing about the subject and describing each step.

10. Not identifying SPECIFIC opportunities to apply the lesson.
If you don't point out specific applications for the lesson, you're like a football coach who gives a rousing pep talk, draws up the plays to run, but does not schedule any games. Point out opportunities in the coming week to apply their knowledge.

11. Failing to model what you teach.
Values are *caught* more often than they are taught. Your walk speaks louder than your talk. When reading the book of Judges, you will notice that each time a leader died, the people fell right back into sin. People need leadership **they can see.** They want to know first hand that the Christian life works. As Dr. Max Sturdivant says, "At the end of the day, the life you lead is the real Bible lesson."

12. Resenting challenging questions.
You don't want simpletons who blindly follow everything they hear. The New Testament commends Christians for scrutinizing what the apostles were teaching. *"But the people of Berea were more open minded than those in Thessalonica, and gladly listened to the message. They searched the Scriptures day by day to check up on Paul and Silas' statements to see if they were really so."* (Acts 17:11, TLB) You're trying to develop strong, mature people of God. Paul was not offended by his students' verification of scripture, and neither should we. Don't stiffen up when someone asks a question.

13. Not taking time to think.
If you are asked a question, you should welcome the opportunity to explain your point in more detail. But before you answer, make sure you understand the question and take time to formulate your answer. *"A wise man thinks before he speaks; what he says is then more persuasive."* (Proverbs 16:23) One way to gain a few extra moments to answer is to repeat the question for the class. Remember, *"He that answers a matter before he hears it, it is folly and shame unto him."* (Proverbs 18:13)

14. Favoring certain students.
Adults are quite sensitive to favoritism. There will be certain students who impress you, but be careful not to make the others feel inadequate. Remember Malachi 2:9: *"Therefore I have made you contemptible in the eyes of all the people; for you have not obeyed me, but you let **your favorites** break the law without rebuke."*

15. Not expressing interest in what class members say.
When students volunteer comments, encourage them by your eye contact and undivided attention. Your facial expressions will convey either interest or apathy. A smile is worth a thousand words.

16. Bad breath.
As a teacher, you will be in close proximity to members of your class. Bad breath distracts from your effectiveness. Before going to class, use mouthwash or peppermints. In fact, putting some mints in your car is a great idea.

17. Teaching too long.
A good thing taken to extremes can be bad. Because of your passion and extensive preparation, it is easy to *over* teach by:

a. Exceeding your students' physical endurance. After an hour, students comprehend about 17% of what they hear. Although Paul said *"I kept back nothing that was helpful,"* he did not teach them everything at one time. If you reach the end of the class period without completing the lesson, simply finish it next week. Even the Lord had limits on how much he taught:
"For I have given to them the words which You have given Me." **(and no more)** (John 17:8) Note the wise counsel of Proverbs 30:5-6: *"Every word of God is pure: he is a shield unto them that put their trust in him.* **Add you not unto his words."**

b. Exceeding their receptivity to your lesson. Your students are at various points in their spiritual journeys. Because of this, most will receive basic points more easily than advanced teachings. Don't go further than they are able to accept. The Lord taught *"as much as they were ready to understand."* (Mark 4:33, TLB) Realistically gauge the *"spiritual temperature"* of your class and *"stretch"* as much as you can without losing them.

18. Not maintaining confidentiality.

If a member of your class asks for prayer about a sensitive matter, do not splash the information all over the church. This is no more than gossiping. And if you are a gossip, you cannot be trusted with a secret. (Proverbs 11:13) **Being a gossip disqualifies a person from being a teacher:** *"Wicked men spread gossip; they stir up trouble and break up friendships."* (Proverbs 16:28)

19. "Talking down" to the class.

There is a difference between teaching on an appropriate level and teaching in a condescending manner. Don't underestimate your students.

20. Appearing arrogant.

Although the roles of the teacher and student are different, both are equal in value. Every good teacher knows that the true Teacher is the Holy Spirit and that He is responsible for any good that comes from the lesson. In the words of Dr. K. Webb, "The work of the Holy Spirit flows around and through every aspect of teaching. If you forget the Holy Spirit, you're dead."

21. Letting the Sunday School Quarterly (or any other set program) preclude discussion over momentous events and tragedies.

If a major event has occurred in the community or the nation, the teacher needs to set aside the lesson plan for the day. It is a time for prayer, sharing and comfort.

22. Not paying attention to their facial expressions and body language.

Students who look bored probably are. Pick up on this and change something. Do **not** continue what you were doing.

23. Not paying attention to your own facial expression and body language.

Conversely, let your expressions reflect enthusiasm. Students will be motivated by your interest in them.

24. Not appreciating the value of entertainment.

There is nothing wrong with entertainment. People won't come if they don't enjoy it! DON'T BORE THEM!

25. Not conditioning students to listen to key facts.

Tell them what's important; which things are key. Illuminate the theme and put it in context. They need to know **why** and **how** something affects them.

26. Not knowing their names.

Learn your student's names. If necessary, use name tags. "I have called you by your name." (Isaiah 43:1)

27. Not realizing that the message you have is far better than any other event, activity, or experience your students could have.

Your lessons have eternal significance and will change their lives forever.

28. Teaching without a story.

Everyone likes a story. Relive it as you tell it.

29. Teaching without passion.

Nothing great was ever done without enthusiasm.

30. Teaching without an outline.

If you're not organized, you're not teaching. Do not leave any room for your students to get off track.

Chapter 20

Know Your Own Teaching Style

Which teaching profile is yours? What are your tendencies?

1. **SIMON PETER.** *"Be it far from you, Lord: this shall not be unto you."* (Matt 16:22)
   A. Passionate leader.
   B. Concerned with the "here and now."
   C. Emotional and impulsive. (Occasionally hot tempered).
   D. *NEEDS to exercise judgment and self-control and should:*
      1. Take time to reflect on the situation.
      2. Read commentaries before teaching to grasp the larger issue.
      3. Spend time in prayer every morning.
      4. Avoid getting off track because of your powerful influence over others. "I go a fishing. They say unto him, We also go with you." (John 21:3)

2. **JOHN the BAPTIST** *"For John had said unto Herod, It is not lawful for you ..."* (Mk 6:18)
   A. Is **not** concerned with what others think.
   B. Is concerned with righteousness. Intimate and powerful relationship with God.
   C. Works best alone.
   D. Visionary leader.
   E. *NEEDS to include lighthearted fun in the Sunday School experience and should:*
      1. Ask someone to be the class event planner for activities and social events.
      2. Use tasteful humor occasionally.
      3. Mingle with others before class.
      4. Ask class members to read, pray, and give praise reports.
      5. Phone class members occasionally for purely social reasons.
      6. Share his everyday challenges to avoid seeming impersonal.
      7. Not "preach people out of church."

3. **The ANGEL GABRIEL** *"I am Gabriel, that stand in the presence of God; and am sent to speak unto you."* (Luke 1:19)
   A. Final authority, unyielding.
   B. Things seem clear and obvious.
   C. Is **not** receptive to excuses.
   D. *NEEDS to understand that the teacher and the student are of equal value and should:*
      1. Be aware of his own body language and smile more often.
      2. Not overreact to mistakes.
      3. Realize that we are all fallible.

4. **The APOSTLE PAUL.** *"You even owe me your very soul!"* (Philemon 1:19, TLB)
   A. Relationship-oriented.
   B. Seeks to be doctrinally correct and truthful.
   D. Seeks the support of the church administration. Likes to have authority.
   D. Aggressive, outspoken.
   E. Visionary.
   F. Change catalyst. Likes forward progress.
   G. Puts all that he is into the class.
   H. Willing to sacrifice everything for knowing God.
   I. Expects everyone to get on board voluntarily, but will urge fervently if they don't.
   J. Gifted. Highly educated. Hard working.
   K. *NEEDS to beware of becoming arrogant and impatient and should:*
      1. Be thankful and joyful about suffering and challenges along the way.
      2. Not allow demanding projects to take priority over pure faith.
      3. Communicate in plain, simple ways.
      4. Realize that others treasure his words of encouragement and approval.

Chapter 21

Sample Lesson: God's Will

Part 1: SEED

Biblical definition contrasted with the world's definition.

- We are going to talk about a wonderful topic this morning: God's will.
- There is a lot of misunderstanding about this subject, so I want to explain what God's will is and what it is not.

God's will is that which he desires and ordains for you.

"For I know the thoughts that I think toward you, says the Lord, thoughts of peace, and not of evil, to give you an expected end." (Jeremiah 29:11)

The will of God is that you conduct yourself like one of His children.

"For you were sometimes darkness, but now are you light in the Lord: walk as children of light: (For the fruit of the Spirit is in all goodness and righteousness and truth;) Proving what is acceptable unto the Lord." (Ephesians 5:8-10)

God's will is expressed in the Bible.

"Your word is a lamp unto my feet, and a light unto my path. I have sworn, and I will perform it, that I will keep your righteous judgments." (Psalms 119: 105-106)

The will of God is opposed to the conduct of the world.

- *"And have no fellowship with the unfruitful works of darkness, but rather reprove them. For it is a shame even to speak of those things which are done of them in secret."* (Eph 5:11, 12)
- *"Don't copy the behavior and customs of this world, but be a new and different person with a fresh newness in all you do and think. Then you will learn from your own experience how his ways will really satisfy you."* (Romans 12:2, The Living Bible)
- *"Know you not that the friendship of the world is enmity with God? Whosoever therefore will be a friend of the world is the enemy of God. Do you think that the scripture says in vain, The spirit that dwells in us lusts to envy?"* (James 4:4-5)

Many people think the Lord is not concerned about their conduct and that they can do whatever they want. Whoever heard of a Father who didn't care what his children did?

- *"The eyes of the Lord are in every place, beholding the evil and the good."* (Proverbs 15:3)
- *"I will search with lanterns in Jerusalem's darkest corners to find and punish those who sit contented in their sins, indifferent to God, thinking he will let them alone."* (Zephaniah 1:12, TLB)

Part 2: NEED *(Why they need to learn about this topic)*

We have plenty of good reasons to know God's will.

Why should we seek to know God's will?

- **God commands us to know his will.**
  - *"See then that you walk circumspectly, not as fools, but as wise, Redeeming the time, because the days are evil. Wherefore be you not unwise, but understanding what the will of the Lord is."* (Ephesians 5:15-17)
  - *"Be you not as the horse, or as the mule, which have no understanding: whose mouth must be held in with bit and bridle, lest they come near unto thee."* (Psalms 32:9)

- **Knowing and doing the will of God identifies you with God's people.** *"Not every one that says unto me, Lord, Lord, shall enter into the kingdom of heaven; but he that does the will of my Father which is in heaven."* (Jesus, in Matthew 7:21)

- **Knowing and doing God's will shows that you are in Jesus' family.** *"For whosoever shall do the will of my Father which is in heaven, the same is my brother, and sister, and mother."* (Jesus, in Matthew 12:50)

- **God is directing the steps of the upright.** *"A wicked man hardens his face: but as for the upright, he directs his way."* (Proverbs 21:29)

- **Because we cannot plan our own lives. Only God knows the future.** *"Remember the former things of old: for I am God, and there is none else; I am God, and there is none like me, declaring the end from the beginning, and from ancient times the things that are not yet done, saying, My counsel shall stand, and I will do all my pleasure."* (Isaiah 46:9-10)

- **There is happiness and "great reward" in doing God's will.** *"The statutes of the Lord are right, rejoicing the heart: the commandment of the Lord is pure, enlightening the eyes. The fear of the Lord is clean, enduring for ever: the judgments of the Lord are true and righteous altogether. More to be desired are they than gold, yes, than much fine gold: sweeter also than honey and the honeycomb. Moreover by them is your servant warned: and **in keeping of them there is great reward.**"* (Psalm 19:8-11)

Sample Lesson: God's Will

What results from *failing to know* God's will?

✦ **Disobedience and God's Judgment.**

- *"But what can we expect from the poor and ignorant?* **They don't know the ways of God. How can they obey him?** *I will go now to their leaders, the men of importance, and speak to them, for they know the ways of the Lord and the* **judgment that follows sin.** *But they too had utterly rejected their God. So I will send upon them the wild fury of the "lion from the forest;" the "desert wolves" shall pounce upon them, and a "leopard" shall lurk around their cities so that all who go out shall be torn apart."* (Jeremiah 5:4-6)

- *"Let no man deceive you with vain words: for because of these things comes the wrath of God upon the children of disobedience."* (Ephesians 5:6)

✦ **A lack of understanding about God's direction of your life.**

- *"Lord, I know it is not within the power of man to map his life and plan his course- so you correct me, Lord; but please be gentle."* (Jeremiah 10:23)

- *"Live no longer as the unsaved do, for they are blinded and confused. Their closed hearts are full of darkness; they are far away from the life of God because they have shut their minds against him, and they cannot understand his ways. They don't care anymore about right and wrong and have given themselves over to impure ways."* (Ephesians 4:17-19)

Part 3: FEED

Present a well-rounded, logical presentation of the subject. Start with the foundational point and build upon it with more advanced points.

These verses are life-changing. This is some of the best information I have ever come across.

It is easier to understand God's will if we know God's nature.

- *"God is love."* (1 John 4:8)
- **Every good thing comes from God.** *"Whatever is good and perfect comes to us from God, the Creator of all light, and he shines forever without change or shadow."* (James 1:17)
- **God is generous.** *"If you then, being evil, know how to give good gifts unto your children, how much more shall your Father which is in heaven give good things to them that ask him?"* (Matthew 7:11)
- **God is loving and kind.** *"Whoso is wise, and will observe these things, even they shall understand the loving kindness of the Lord."* (Psalms 107:43)
- **God accepts repentance.** *"The sacrifices of God are a broken spirit: a broken and a contrite heart, O God, you will not despise."* (Psalms 51:17)
- **God demands loyalty from us.** *"You shall not bow down yourself to them, nor serve them: for I the Lord thy God am a jealous God."* (Exodus 20:5)
- **God will judge us.** *"For we know him that has said, Vengeance belongs unto me, I will recompense, says the Lord. And again, The Lord shall judge his people. It is a fearful thing to fall into the hands of the living God."* (Hebrews 10:30-31)
- **You can always count on God.** *"Jesus Christ the same yesterday, and to day, and for ever."* (Hebrews 13:8)
- **God is always thinking of you.** *"Behold, I have graven you upon the palms of my hands."* (Isaiah 49:16)
- **God desires the best for us.** *"For I know the plans I have for you, says the Lord. They are plans for good and not for evil, to give you a future and a hope."* (Jeremiah 29:11)

The study of God's will is part of wise living.

- *"See then that you walk circumspectly, not as fools, but as wise, Redeeming the time, because the days are evil. Wherefore **<u>be you not unwise, but understanding what the will of the Lord is</u>**."* (Ephesians 5:15-17)
- *"The fear of the Lord is the beginning of wisdom: a good understanding have all they that do his commandments: his praise endures forever."* (Psalms 111:10)
- <u>Wisdom involves **doing** something</u>. *"And unto man he said, Behold, the fear of the Lord, that is wisdom; and **to depart from evil** is understanding."* (Job 28:28)

"Lip service" and doing God's will are two different things.

A man with two sons told the older boy, 'Son, go out and work on the farm today.' 'I won't,' he answered, but later he changed his mind and went. Then the father told the youngest, 'You go!' and he said, 'Yes, sir, I will.' But he didn't. Which of the two was obeying his father?" They replied, "The first, of course." (Matthew 21:28-31, TLB)

Obedience is God's Will

"Let us hear the conclusion of the whole matter: Fear God, and keep his commandments: for this is the whole duty of man. For God shall bring every work into judgment, with every secret thing, whether it be good or whether it be evil." (Ecclesiastes 12:13-14)

The Lord's will requires all of you.

"And now, Israel, what does the Lord thy God require of you, but to fear the Lord thy God, to walk in all his ways, and to love him, and to serve the Lord your God with all your heart and with all your soul." (Deuteronomy 10:12)

"Jesus said unto him, You shall love the Lord your God with all your heart, and with all your soul, and with all your mind. This is the first and great commandment. And the second is like unto it, You shall love thy neighbor as yourself. On these two commandments hang all the law and the prophets." (Matthew 22:37-40)

We should never be apprehensive about the Lord's will. It is not too difficult. If the Lord directs you, he equips you for the task. (God's will is what everyone would do if they knew all the facts).

✦ *"He has shown you, O man, what is good; and what does the Lord require of you but to do justly, to love mercy, and to walk humbly with your God?"* (Micah 6:8, NKJV)

✦ *"Obeying these commandments is not something beyond your strength and reach."* (Deuteronomy 30:11)

✦ *"Loving God means doing what he tells us to do, and really, that isn't hard at all."* (1 John 5:3, The Living Bible)

In fact, it is much easier to do God's will than not.

✦ *"It is hard for you to kick against the goads."* (Acts 9:5, NKJV)

✦ *"Wear my yoke – for it fits perfectly – and let me teach you; for I am gentle and humble, and you shall find rest for your souls; for I give you only light burdens."*
(Jesus, in Matthew 11:29-30, The Living Bible)

All animals are created to do certain things. For example, a woodpecker is designed to retrieve insects from tree trunks while a pelican is made to pluck fish from the ocean. An ox is built for pulling great weights while a sheep dog enjoys herding livestock in the field. Would you use a sheep dog to pull a plow? Or an ox to herd sheep? It is much more enjoyable to do the work for which you were created. What is your strong suite? ***What comes easy to you? You are designed for a specific purpose.***

God guides us to preserve his good reputation and because he is compassionate.

- *"As a beast goes down into the valley, the Spirit of the Lord caused him to rest: so did you lead thy people, **to make yourself a glorious name**."* (Isaiah 63:14)
- *"For you are my rock and my fortress; therefore **for your name's sake** lead me, and guide me."* (Psalms 31: 3)
- *"But when he saw the multitudes, **he was moved with <u>compassion</u> on them**, because they fainted, and were scattered abroad, as sheep having no shepherd."* (Matthew 9:36)
- *"And the Lord commanded us to do all these statutes, to fear the Lord our God, **for our good** always, that he might preserve us alive, as it is at this day."* (Deuteronomy 6:24)

God's will is much better for us than our own will.

- *"Now unto him that is able to do exceeding abundantly above all that we ask or think, according to the power that works in us."* (Ephesians 3:20)
- *"... how often would I have gathered your children together, even as a hen gathers her chickens under her wings, and you would not!"* (Matthew 23:37)
- *"For my thoughts are not your thoughts, neither are your ways my ways, says the Lord. For as the heavens are higher than the earth, so are **my ways higher than your ways**, and my thoughts than your thoughts."* (Isaiah 55:8, 9)

God's will is obvious.

- **2 Chronicles 32:22**
  *"Thus the Lord saved Hezekiah and the inhabitants of Jerusalem from the hand of Sennacherib the king of Assyria, and from the hand of all other, and **guided them on every side**".*
- **Isaiah 30:21**
  "And your ears shall hear a word behind you, saying, This is the way, walk you in it, when you turn to the right hand, and when you turn to the left."
- **Exodus 13: 21-22**
  *"And the Lord went before them **by day** in a pillar of a cloud, to lead them the way; and **by night** in a pillar of fire, to give them light; to go by day and night: He took not away the pillar of the cloud by day, nor the pillar of fire by night, from before the people."*

Sample Lesson: God's Will

God's guidance is constant.

✦ **Psalm 48:14** *"For this great God is our God forever and ever. He will be our guide until we die."*

✦ **Psalm 73:24.** *"You shall guide me with your counsel, and afterward receive me to glory."*

✦ **John 16:13** *"Howbeit when he, the Spirit of truth, is come, he will guide you into all truth: for he shall not speak of himself; but whatsoever he shall hear, that shall he speak: and **he will show you things to come**."*

God's will may be revealed one step at a time.

✦ **Acts 9:6** *And he trembling and astonished said, Lord, what will you have me to do? And the Lord said unto him, Arise, and go into the city, and it shall be told you what you must do.*

✦ **Remember, even the wise men had to stop to ask directions.** *Now when Jesus was born in Bethlehem of Judaea in the days of Herod the king, behold, there came wise men from the east to Jerusalem, Saying, Where is he that is born King of the Jews? for we have seen his star in the east, and are come to worship him.* (Matthew 2:1-2)

God's will is accompanied by peace.

✦ **Philippians 4:6-7** (The Living Bible) *Don't worry about anything; instead, pray about everything; tell God your needs and don't forget to thank him for his answers. If you do this you will experience God's peace, which is far more wonderful than the human mind can understand. His peace will keep your thoughts and your hearts quiet and at rest as you trust in Christ Jesus.*

✦ **1 Corinthians 7:15** *God has called us to peace.*

✦ **Colossians 3:15** *And let the peace of God rule (be the umpire) in your hearts, to the which also you are called in one body; and be thankful.*

(If you feel uncomfortable or anxious about something, it isn't God's will).

"While he (Pontius Pilate) was sitting on the judgment seat, his wife sent to him, saying, "Have nothing to do with that just Man, for I have suffered many things today in a dream because of Him." (Matthew 27:19, NKJV)

*The king was **grieved**, but because of his oath, and because he didn't want to back down in front of his guests, he issued the necessary orders. So John was beheaded in the prison.* (Matthew 14:9, The Living Bible)

*And a stone was brought, and laid upon the mouth of the den; and the king sealed it with his own signet, and with the signet of his lords; that the purpose might not be changed concerning Daniel. Then the king went to his palace, and passed the night fasting: neither were instruments of music brought before him: and **his sleep went from him**.* (Daniel 6:17-18)

Questions for Determining if an Opportunity is God's will:

- Does it honor God?
- Is it Scriptural? If it goes against the Bible's teachings, it is not God's will.
- Would you feel confident in asking Jesus to help you accomplish it? If not, drop it.
- Do you have the **time** to do it? (Would it deprive you of time with your family for an extended period? Would it deprive you of rest for an extended period?) To prevent stress, if you add one project, you should drop another. Are you willing to give up something to have the time to do it?
- Do you have the **money** to do it? God often leads us by providing or withholding financial support. If God wants you to do it, he will provide the means.
- Do you have the **desire** to do it? God gives us wholesome, noble, and exciting goals.
- Do you have the **talent** to do it? Don't fight the facts of nature. If you are short and stocky, it is not likely that God wants you to play professional basketball.
- Is the investment, or its price, above normal? Does the price make you uneasy? Do you feel that it would be a wise use of **the Lord's** money?
- Would it help others?
- Would it **hurt** someone else?
- Is it profitable? Generally speaking, God's will is good and helpful to you. You don't have extra time in this life to waste on projects that don't produce. *"All things are lawful, but not all things are profitable.* (I Cor.10:23 - NASB)
- Have you prayed about it? (Before you pray, **don't have an opinion**, but be equally happy for God to say "no" or "yes.") Remember, if God denies your request, *it is always to give you something much better.*
- Do you feel at **peace** about it? We are called to peace.
- Would you feel at peace if God said "no," or "not now."
- **Go where the evidence leads.** Don't go by what people say, but rather what they do. Are other wise Christians doing it? Are they investing as much time and energy as you are considering? Remember that people encouraging you to do something wrong will back away from you if you do it.
- If you did it, **what would it mean for you in one year**? **Five years**?
- If you did not do it, where will you be down the road? For example, if you choose not to go to law school, where will you be three years from now without a law degree?
- Do you feel **pressured** to do it *now*? Does this make you feel uncomfortable or unsure?
- Would you be **fully happy** if you did not do it, or will you regret it later in life?
- Are you hesitating because you are comfortable with where you are? Nehemiah was comfortable in the king's palace, but chose to go where work needed to be done.
- Have you researched the matter thoroughly? Have you taken time to "do the math?" Collect plenty of detailed data. Know what you're getting in to. Get the facts. Disregard appearances.
- Have you talked to someone who is already successful at what you want to do?
- Don't be scared to obey. Remember that the Lord will not let you starve. *"I have been young, and now am old; yet have I not seen the righteous forsaken, nor his seed begging bread."* (Psalm 37:25)
- Are you hesitating because **your spouse** is leery? The definition of a visionary leader is that he knows what the outcome is supposed to look like. Don't expect others to understand your passion at first. *"And unto Adam he said, Because you have hearkened unto the voice of your wife, … in sorrow shall you eat of it all the days of thy life."* (Genesis 3:17)
- Ask the question: "What would Jesus do?"
- Don't listen to the crowd.
- Don't listen to peers. Let me say again, **don't listen to peers.** They may be envious.
- Does it bring glory to God?

Sample Lesson: God's Will

Part 4: DEED

Apply your knowledge today.

All of our learning is for nothing if we don't apply the lesson. Remember, the blessing is in the doing. *"a doer of the work, this man shall be blessed in his deed."* (James 1:25)

Pray for God to lead you.

- (Psalm 25:5) *Lead me in your truth, and teach me: for you are the God of my salvation; on you do I wait all the day.*

- (Matthew 6:13) *And lead us not into temptation, but deliver us from evil.*

- (Psalm 43:3) *O send out your light and thy truth: let them lead me; let them bring me unto your holy hill, and to your tabernacles.*

- (James 1:5) *If any of you lack wisdom,* **let him ask of God**, *that gives to all men liberally, and upbraids not; and it shall be given him.*

- (Isaiah 40:11) *He shall feed his flock like a shepherd: he shall gather the lambs with his arm, and carry them in his bosom, and shall gently lead those that are with young.*

- Isaiah 42:16 *And I will bring the blind by a way that they knew not;* **I will lead them** *in paths that they have not known: I will make darkness light before them, and crooked things straight.*

Expect God to lead you skillfully.

- *You shall guide* **me** *with your counsel.* (Psalm 73:24)

- *I will instruct you and teach you in the way which you shall go: I will guide you with my eye.* (Psalms 32:8-9)

- *But made his own people to go forth like sheep, and guided them in the wilderness like a flock.* (Psalm 78:52)

- *So he fed them according to the integrity of his heart; and guided them* **by the skillfulness of his hands**. (Psalms 78:72)

Expect your path to become clearer and clearer.

- *But the path of the just is as the shining light, that shines more and more unto the perfect day.* (Proverbs 4:18)

- **Obedience to God's direction brings more detailed understanding.** *And he said to them, Follow me, and I will make you fishers of men. And they straightway left their nets, and followed him.* (Matthew 4: 19-20)

Put God first in your life.

- Proverbs 3:6 *In all your ways acknowledge him, and he shall direct your paths.*

- Isaiah 58:10-11 The Living Bible *Feed the hungry! Help those in trouble!* **Then** *your light will shine out from the darkness, and the darkness around you shall be as bright as day. And the Lord will guide you* **continually**, *and satisfy you with all good things, and keep you healthy too; and you will be like a well-watered garden, like an ever flowing spring. Your sons will rebuild the long-deserted ruins of your cities, and you will be known as "The People Who Rebuild Their Walls and Cities."*

- Psalm 139:24 *And see if there be any wicked way in me, and lead me in the way everlasting.*

- Psalm 25:12-13 *What man is <u>he that fears the Lord</u>? Him shall he teach in the way that he shall choose. His soul shall dwell at ease; and his seed shall inherit the earth.*

- Psalm 37:23 *The steps of a good man are ordered by the Lord: and he delights in his way.*

- Psalm 25:9-10 *The meek will he guide in judgment: and the meek will he teach his way. All the paths of the Lord are mercy and truth unto such as keep his covenant and his testimonies.*

Practical Application

- Identify one thing that you are considering doing (even if it is a small matter).

- Pray for God's wisdom. *"If any of you lack wisdom, let him ask of God, that gives to all men liberally, and upbraids not; and it shall be given him."* (James 1:5)

- Research and analyze the opportunity in the light of these scriptures.

- Reach a decision.

- If you have peace about your choice, take action.

Chapter 22

Sample Lesson: Freedom from Sin

Part 1: SEED (Definition)

For all have sinned, and come short of the glory of God. (Romans 3:23)

Sin is anything that does not meet God's standards. Some think that anything you do is alright as long as you are sincere. In the ancient Greek, the term for this was "horse feathers."

Where does sin originate? The human heart.
- *And God saw that the wickedness of man was great in the earth, and that every imagination of the thoughts of his heart was only evil continually.* (Genesis 6:5)
- *The heart is deceitful above all things, and desperately wicked: who can know it?* (Jeremiah 17:9)

Sin takes three basic forms:
the lust of the flesh, the lust of the eyes, and pride.

For all that is in the world, the lust of the flesh, and the lust of the eyes, and the pride of life, is not of the Father, but is of the world. (1 John 2:16) Lust is a strong desire or passion for something.
For example, greed is an excessive, unending drive to accumulate.

The lust of the flesh *(The desires of the body)*	The lust of the eyes *(Get, get, get)*	The pride of life *(Arrogance, self-centeredness)*
1. Consuming too much. (gluttony, drunkenness). Luke 21:34. *And take heed to yourselves, lest at any time your hearts be overcharged with overeating, and drunkenness, and cares of this life, and so that day come upon you unawares.*	**1. Wanting whatever you see. (Theft, covetousness, neighbor's spouse)** Luke 7:21-22. *For from within, out of the heart of men, proceed evil thoughts, adulteries, fornications, murders, thefts, <u>covetousness</u>, wickedness, deceit, lasciviousness, an evil eye, blasphemy, pride, foolishness:*	**1. Arrogance.** Proverbs 21:4 *An high look, and a proud heart, and the plowing of the wicked, is sin.* Proverbs 26:12 *Do you see a man wise <u>in his own conceit</u>? there is more hope of a fool than of him.*
2. Illicit sexual relations or desires. Matthew 5:27-28 *You have heard that it was said by them of old time, You shall not commit adultery: But I say unto you, That whosoever looks on a woman to lust after her has committed adultery with her already in his heart.*	**2. Wanting others possessions enough to kill to get them.** James 4:1-2, TLB: *What is causing the quarrels and fights among you? Isn't it because there is a whole army of evil desires within you? You want what you don't have, so you kill to get it. <u>You long for what others have</u>, and can't afford it, so you start a fight to take it away from them.*	**2. Desire to take God's place.** Isaiah 14:13-14. *For you have said in your heart, I will ascend into heaven, I will exalt my throne above the stars of God: I will sit also upon the mount of the congregation, in the sides of the north: I will ascend above the heights of the clouds; I will be like the most High.*
3. Laziness, sleeping too much. Proverbs 6:9-11. *How long will you sleep, <u>O sluggard</u>? When will you arise out of your sleep? Yet a little sleep, a little slumber, a little folding of the hands to sleep: So shall your poverty come as one that travels, and your want as an armed man.*	**3. Greed.** Proverbs 1:18-19: *And they lay wait for their own blood; they lurk privily for their own lives. So are the ways of every one that is greedy of gain; which takes away the life of the owners thereof.* Isaiah 56:11: *Yes, they are greedy dogs which <u>can never have enough</u>, and they are shepherds that cannot understand: they all look to their own way, every one for his gain, from his quarter.*	**3. Rebellion.** Jeremiah 29:32. *Therefore thus says the Lord; Behold, I will punish Shemaiah the Nehelamite, and his seed: he shall not have a man to dwell among this people; neither shall he behold the good that I will do for my people, says the Lord; because he has taught rebellion against the Lord.*

Part 2: NEED

The consequences of sin are devastating. The story of Samson illustrates this. He was betrayed, blinded, bound, and belittled.
If you don't defeat sin, sin will defeat you.

Do we suffer for sinning?

- *But he that does wrong **shall receive for the wrong** which he has done: and there is no respect of persons.* (Colossians 3:25)
- *Be not deceived; God is not mocked: for whatsoever a man plants, that shall he also reap.* (Galatians 6:7)
- *Mortify therefore your members which are upon the earth; fornication, uncleanness, inordinate affection, evil concupiscence, and covetousness, which is idolatry: For which things' sake **the wrath of God comes** on the children of disobedience.* (Colossians 3:5-6)

How do we suffer for our sins?

1. Physical problems.

- *Afterward Jesus finds him in the temple, and said unto him, Behold, you are made whole: sin no more, **lest a worse thing come unto you.*** (John 5:14)
- *And David said unto Nathan, I have sinned against the Lord. And Nathan said unto David, The Lord also has put away your sin; you shall not die. Howbeit, because by this deed you have given great occasion to the enemies of the Lord to blaspheme, **the child also that is born unto you shall surely die.*** (2 Samuel 12:13-14)
- *There is **no soundness in my flesh** because of your anger; **neither is there any rest** in my bones because of my sin.* (Psalm 38:3)

2. Shame.

- *The wise shall inherit glory: but **shame** shall be the promotion of fools.* (Proverbs 3:35)
- *Righteousness exalts a nation: but <u>sin is a reproach</u> to any people.* (Proverbs 14:34)

3. Bondage: Loss of Freedom.

- *Don't you realize that you can choose your own master? You can choose sin (with death) or else obedience (with acquittal). **The one to whom you offer yourself** - he will take you and be your master and you will be his slave.* (Romans 6:16 TLB)
- *Know you not, that to whom **you yield yourselves** servants to obey, his servants you are to whom you obey; whether of sin unto death, or of obedience unto righteousness?* (Romans 6:16)
- *Jesus answered them, Verily, verily, I say unto you, Whosoever **commits** sin is the servant of sin.* (John 8:34)

4. Spiritual Blindness.

✦ *The way of the wicked is as darkness: they know not at what they stumble.* (Proverbs 4:19)
✦ *And she said, The Philistines be upon thee, Samson. And He awoke out of his sleep, and said, I will go out as at other times before, and shake myself. And he wist not that the Lord was departed from him. But the Philistines took him, and **put out his eyes**, and brought him down to Gaza, and bound him with fetters of brass; and he did grind in the prison house.* (Judges 16:20-21)
✦ *Let me say this, then, speaking for the Lord: Live no longer as the unsaved do, for **they are blinded and confused**.* (Ephesians 4:17, TLB)
✦ *In whom the god of this world has **blinded the minds** of them which believe not.* (2 Corinthians 4:4)

5. Demotion and financial loss.

✦ *And Saul said unto Samuel, I have sinned: for I have transgressed the commandment of the Lord, and your words: because I feared the people, and obeyed their voice. Now therefore, I pray thee, pardon my sin, and turn again with me, that I may worship the Lord. And Samuel said unto Saul, I will not return with you: for you have rejected the word of the Lord, and the Lord has rejected thee from being king over Israel. And as Samuel turned about to go away, he laid hold upon the skirt of his mantle, and it rent. And Samuel said unto him, The Lord has rent the kingdom of Israel from you this day, and **has given it to a neighbor of yours, that is better than you.*** (1 Samuel 15:24-28)
✦ *Remove your way far from her, and come not near the door of her house: Lest you give your honor unto others, and your years unto the cruel: Lest strangers be filled with your wealth; and your labors be in the house of a stranger.* (Proverbs 5:8-10)
✦ *The wealth of the sinner is laid up for the just.* (Proverbs 13:22)

6. Lost opportunities and blessings.

✦ ***When I would have healed Israel**, then the iniquity of Ephraim was discovered, and the wickedness of Samaria: for they commit falsehood; and the thief comes in, and the troop of robbers spoils without. And they consider not in their hearts that I remember all their wickedness: now their own doings have beset them about; they are before my face.* (Hosea 7:1-2)
✦ ***How often would I have gathered thy children together**, even as a hen gathers her chickens under her wings, and you would not!* (Jesus, in Matthew 23:37)

7. Distance from God.

✦ *Woe unto them! for **they have fled from me**: destruction unto them! because they have transgressed against me.* (Hosea 7:13)
✦ *Behold, the Lord's hand is not shortened, that it cannot save; neither his ear heavy, that it cannot hear: But your iniquities have separated between you and your God, and **your sins have hid his face** from you, that he will not hear.* (Isaiah 59:1-2)

Part 3: FEED
Progressive modules on how to avoid sin.

1. **Read and know the Bible.** *Your word have I hid in my heart, that I might not sin against thee.* (Psalm 119:11)

2. **Believe that you are dead to sin. Stop struggling and start believing!**
I am crucified with Christ: nevertheless I live; yet not I, but Christ lives in me: and the life which I now live in the flesh I live by the faith of the Son of God, who loved me, and gave himself for me. (Galatians 2:20)

Your old evil desires were nailed to the cross with him; that part of you that loved to sin was crushed and fatally wounded, so that your sin-loving body is no longer under sin's control, no longer needs to be a slave to sin; for when you are deadened to sin you are freed from all its allure and its power over you. (Romans 6:6-7)

There was a dog that, for years, was kept in his yard by an invisible electrical pulsating fence. One day the owner turned off the electric fence. The dog was free to explore the neighborhood, but he remained right there in his yard. You see, the pet was not convinced that he was free. Some Christians are like that. They don't reckon (accept as true) that they are free to live a godly life. The problem is not one of will power, but of **accepting** what Christ has already done for us **to be true**. *"***Reckon** *also yourselves to be dead indeed unto sin, but alive unto God through Jesus Christ our Lord."* (Rom 6:11)

Realize what Christ has done for you.
* *The next day John saw Jesus coming unto him, and said, Behold the Lamb of God, which takes away the sin of the world.* (John 1:12)
* *For sin shall not have dominion over you: for you are not under the law, but under grace.* (Romans 6:14)
* The Hebrew translation of "repent" was "to be sorry for." The New Testament translation means "to turn around." We now have power **not** to sin. Jesus' sacrifice repurchased us and returned us to our original state with God.

3. **Pray.** *Pray that you enter not into temptation.* (Luke 22:40)
Watch and pray, that you enter not into temptation: the spirit indeed is willing, but the flesh is weak. (Matthew 26:41)

4. **Don't talk so much.**
In the multitude of words there wants not sin: but he that refrains his lips is wise. (Proverbs 10:19)

Keep your foot when you go to the house of God, and be more ready to hear, than to give the sacrifice of fools (talk): for they consider not that they do evil. Be not rash with your mouth, and let not your heart be hasty to utter any thing before God: for God is in heaven, and you upon earth: therefore **let your words be few***. For a dream comes through the multitude of business; and* **a fool's voice is known by multitude of words***.* (Ecclesiastes 5:1-3)

5. **Don't get close to the sin. Stay clear.**
Run from her! Don't go near her house, *lest you fall to her temptation and lose your honor, and give the remainder of your life to the cruel and merciless; lest strangers obtain your wealth, and you become a slave of foreigners.* (Proverbs 5:7-9 TLB)

Abstain from all appearance of evil. (1 Thessalonians 5:22)

6. **Fear the Lord.** *Let not your heart envy sinners: but be in the fear of the Lord all the day long.* (Proverbs 23:17)

And if you call on the Father, who without respect of persons judges according to every man's work, pass the time of your sojourning here in fear. (1 Peter 1:17)

7. **Stay in fellowship with other Christians.** Wolves attack sheep who are apart from the flock.
Not forsaking the assembling of ourselves together, as the manner of some is; but exhorting one another: and so much the more, as you see the day approaching. (Hebrews 10:25)

Speaking to yourselves in psalms and hymns and spiritual songs, singing and making melody in your heart to the Lord. (Ephesians 5:19)

8. **Learn to "Ride the Wave."** *Temptation is like an ocean wave that continues to grow as it approaches. But as it reaches shore, it crashes and subsides. Hang on until the temptation disintegrates.* **Blessed is the man that endures temptation.** (James 1:12) **Trust, don't taste.**

Sample Lesson: Freedom From Sin

Part 4: DEED
Applying the steps to be free from sin.

✦ Name a place or an activity that you need to avoid in order to avoid temptation.

✦ Name a substitute route or activity that will allow you to avoid the area of temptation.

✦ Have you considered the consequences of sinful activity in this area of temptation? What are they?

✦ Do your attitudes about this danger area stand up to the scrutiny of your Christian friends?

✦ Have you known anyone who became entangled in this area of temptation? What resulted?

✦ How does the fear of the Lord keep you from committing sin?

✦ What would you lose if you sinned in this area?

✦ How would God bless you if you overcame this temptation? **Blessed is the man that endures temptation**: *for when he is tried, he shall receive the crown of life, which the Lord has promised to them that love him.* (James 1:12)

Chapter 23

Sample Lesson: Spiritual Warfare

Upon this rock I will build my church; and the gates of hell shall not prevail against it. (Jesus, in Matthew 16:18)

Part 1: SEED
Biblical Definition

What is spiritual warfare?

Spiritual Warfare is the conflict between God's kingdom and Satan's hierarchy **which God has already won.** It is not a war fought with visible, physical arsenals, but rather with spiritual plans, methods, and weaponry.

From time to time, in the line of duty, police officers break through locked doors. To do this, they use what they call the "master key." The master key is a steel battering ram with several handles on it. In spiritual warfare, our battering ram to destroy the gates of hell is the authority, or name, of Jesus. Thankfully, our Lord outranks every other name and authority, for his name is *"Far above all principality, and power, and might, and dominion, and **every name** that is named, not only in this world, but also in that which is to come: And has put all things under his feet."* (Ephesians 1:21-22)

In Ephesians 6:12, Paul tells us that *"we wrestle not against flesh and blood, but against principalities, against powers, against the rulers of the darkness of this world, against **spiritual wickedness** in high places."* From this scripture, we see that our spiritual enemies are not physical beings, but rather evil spirits. **We cannot hit them or wrestle them physically.** Paul points out, *"I don't use human plans and methods to win my battles. I use God's mighty weapons, not those made by men, to knock down the devil's strongholds."* (2 Corinthians 10:4)

Since Paul called them **"mighty weapons,"** we know that we have a powerful arsenal against the devil and his demons. Jesus also stated that the Christian church will go on the attack and hell will not be able to stop us. *"Upon this rock I will build my church; and the gates of hell shall not prevail against it."* (Matthew 16:18) Our victory is already guaranteed.

One day a middle school invited a policeman to bring his police dog to the campus. So, the tall, sharp policeman brought the animal to the school playground. He let the dog roam for a few minutes and then asked the school children to bring him back. The children dove into their assignment with excitement, running after the sleek animal with delight. However, the canine eluded them easily and continued to roam freely. The dog refused to answer their screams or accept their bribes of candy. In fact, he knocked over a trash can, spilling garbage on the lawn. When the schoolmates were at a loss to retrieve the frolicking beast, the policeman reached into his shirt pocket and pulled out a whistle. The dog recognized the high frequency tone immediately and returned to be leashed. Why did the policeman succeed where the others had failed? He knew which instrument to use. So it is with us. We need to know that, although the devil ignores bodily strength, human intelligence, and negotiation, **he must recognize and obey the authority, or name, of Jesus Christ**. And, like the policeman in the story, we need to know which weapons work and how to use them.

Sample Lesson: Spiritual Warfare

Part 2: NEED

Why should we become skillful in spiritual warfare?

Peter instructs us to *"Be sober, be vigilant; because your adversary the devil walks about like a roaring lion, seeking whom he may devour."* (1 Peter 5:8, NKJV) Notice what Peter is saying:

✦ Satan is *"your adversary."* Satan is already your adversary! Right now, he hates you because it is his permanent nature to hate you.

✦ The devil *"walks about."* Satan is on the prowl, patrolling for an opportunity to steal, kill, and destroy. He wants you to drop your guard. In a word, he is **relentless**.

✦ The devil is *"seeking whom he may devour."* Satan is looking for someone with a weak spot. He is seeking whoever will allow him (through a lack of defense) to come in and destroy. Christians who are out of fellowship with other believers are a preferred prey. He wants to separate you from the flock. Proverbs 6:26 tells us that evil *"will hunt for the precious life."* In other words, a strong Christian would be a prized trophy. The devil is a predator: a financial predator, a sexual predator, and a predator of your well-being.

. . . .

In Numbers 23, there is a story about a prophet who was hired by Moabite princes to curse the Israelites. However, the prophet was unable to fulfill his task because the Israelites were living in God's will. Their lifestyle did not leave any place for a curse to land, thus the prophet replied "How shall I curse, whom God has not cursed? Or how shall I defy, whom the Lord has not defied?" From this story, we see that a godly life is a defense against spiritual attacks.

What benefits will you receive from being trained in spiritual warfare?

✦ **Satan will not gain an advantage over you.** Following the teachings of Christ prevents the devil from gaining an advantage over us. Paul wrote, *"To whom you forgive any thing, I forgive also: for if I forgave any thing, to whom I forgave it, for your sakes forgave I it in the person of Christ; Lest Satan should get an advantage of us: for we are not ignorant of his devices."* (2 Corinthians 2:10, 11)

✦ **You will defeat the devil.** The normal result of our actions is victory. *"I write unto you, young men, because you have overcome the wicked one."* (1 John 2:13)

✦ **Your earnings will be protected.** *"And I will rebuke the devourer for your sakes, and he shall not destroy the fruits of your ground; neither shall your vine cast her fruit before the time in the field, says the Lord of hosts."* (Malachi 3:11)

✦ **You will enjoy a good reputation.** *"And all nations shall call you blessed: for you shall be a delightsome land, says the Lord of hosts."* (Malachi 3:12)

- **You shall be protected from malicious predators.** Jesus said, *"Behold (take this to heart), I give unto you power to tread on serpents and scorpions, and over **all** the power of the enemy: and **nothing shall by any means hurt you.**"* (Luke 10:19)

What are the consequences of being unprepared?

- **Bondage.** The Bible tells us that we are at risk of falling into bondage through sin. Romans 6:16 tells us *"Don't you realize that you can choose your own master? You can choose sin (with death) or else obedience (with acquittal). The one to whom you offer yourself-**he will take you** and be your master and you will be his slave."* In other words, you can choose your own ruler: God or Satan. However, Satan is a cruel task master who seeks your ruin.

- **Destruction.** Paul encouraged his dear friend Timothy to *"wage the good (spiritual) warfare, having faith and a good conscience, which some having rejected, concerning the faith have suffered shipwreck."* (1 Timothy 1:18, 19) The apostle was warning against a "shipwreck" of the soul through failing to engage in spiritual warfare. It is a term describing a state of devastation, uselessness and ruin.

- **Being Deceived.** Satan has deceived people beginning with Eve in the Garden of Eden. Paul wrote that he was very concerned about the Church being duped. *"I fear, lest by any means, as the serpent beguiled Eve through his subtlety, so your minds should be corrupted from the simplicity that is in Christ."* (2 Corinthians 11:3) **Satan is subtle**, which means he is not direct or obvious in his approach. The devil and his emissaries have worked their schemes for thousands of years and are quite refined in their techniques. They don't ring your doorbell and introduce themselves as your enemies from hell. They slip in through the internet, television and mail and they place themselves along your paths.
Paul described the sorcerer in Acts 13:10, as *"**full of all subtlety** and all mischief."* If you fail to remain vigilant, your chances of being deceived increase. Paul was astonished that Christians could become confused about the gospel and wrote, *"O foolish Galatians, **who** has bewitched you, that you should not obey the truth?"* Notice that Paul asks **who**, not what, has deceived them.

Sample Lesson: Spiritual Warfare

Part 3: FEED
Description of spiritual warfare.

Mighty Allies and Resources for Spiritual Warfare:

1. The authority of the King of Kings: Jesus Christ.

Dean Sherman, in his informative book, **Spiritual Warfare for Every Christian**, points out that Satan's greatest fear is that **you will come into the assurance of your authority** and walk in that assurance. What authority? Your authority over the devil and his demons. When did we receive authority? In Luke 10:17-19: *"And the seventy returned again with joy, saying, Lord, even the devils are subject unto us through your name. And he said unto them, I beheld Satan as lightning fall from heaven. Behold, I give unto you power to tread on serpents and scorpions, and* **over all the power of the enemy***: and nothing shall by any means hurt you."* Understand that this is your position as a member of God's royal family, *"because your names are written in heaven."* (Luke 10:20)

And these signs shall follow them that believe; In my name (with my authority) shall they cast out devils. (Mark 16:17)

When we exercise our God-given authority on earth, Jesus *guarantees* to enforce our commands with all the power of heaven: *"Whatsoever you shall bind on earth shall be bound in heaven: and whatsoever you shall loose on earth shall be loosed in heaven."* (Matthew 16:19)

Furthermore, Jesus clearly said that using our authority is our **first** step in spiritual warfare. Before we can invade enemy strongholds, we must first displace Satan. *"No man can enter into a strong man's house (the devil's house), and spoil his goods, except he will* **first** *bind the strong man; and then he will spoil his house."* (Mark 3:27) Remember the famous leader Gideon. Before he embarked on his great military campaign against the Midianites, God required him to *"throw down the altar of Baal that your father has, and cut down the grove that is by it: And build an altar unto the Lord your God upon the top of this rock."* (Judges 6:25-26) In other words, you have to clear out the evil first before you can replace it with God's work.

How do you do this? **Verbally.** Command the devil to leave, just as Jesus did in Matthew 4:10: *"Then **said** Jesus unto him ..."* In Revelation 2:16, Jesus fights with "The sword of my mouth." Revelation 19:21 tells us "the remnant were slain with the sword of him that sat upon the horse, which **sword proceeded out of his mouth.** Our spoken words, in Christ's name, are powerful weapons! *"And they overcame him by the blood of the Lamb, and by the word of their testimony; and they loved not their lives unto death."* (Revelation 12:11)

Where can you send demons?

- **Through dry places.** *"When the unclean spirit is gone out of a man, he walks **through dry places**, seeking rest, and finds none."* (Matthew 12:43)
- **Away out of the country.** *"And he asked him, What is your name? And he answered, saying, My name is Legion: for we are many. And he besought him much that he would not send them **away out of the country**."* (Mark 5:9-10)
- **Into the deep (the abyss, the bottomless pit).** *And they besought him that he would not command them to go out into **the deep**.* (Luke 8:31)

Matthew 12:44-45 reveals that banished demons desire to return with other devils who are more evil than themselves. *"Then he said, I will return into my house from whence I came out; and when he is come, he finds it empty, swept, and garnished. Then goes he, and takes with himself seven other spirits more wicked than himself, and they enter in and dwell there."* So, in addition to casting out the demon, command that he **not return or retaliate**. Furthermore, fill the void left by the demon with God's Holy Spirit. "I charge you, come out of him, and enter no more." (Mark 9:25)

2. Prayer.

John Wesley, the founder of the Methodist church, said *"God does nothing, except by prayer."* Jesus commanded, *"Watch and pray, that you enter not into temptation."* Life's victories are won during our quiet hours of morning prayer and Bible reading. **Never begin more projects than you can pray about.**

- *"You have not, because you ask not."* (James 4:2)

- *"The effectual fervent prayer of a righteous man avails much."* (James 5:16)

- *"Then said he (an angel) unto me, Fear not, Daniel: for from the first day that you did set your heart to understand, and to chasten yourself before thy God, your words were heard, and I am come for your words."* (Daniel 10:12)

- *When I cry unto you, then shall my enemies turn back.* (Psalm 56:9)

3. The Word of Your Testimony.

*And they overcame him by the blood of the Lamb, and by **the word of their testimony**.* (Revelation 12:11) It is important to both know and to profess our true identity. We are kings and priests unto God and members of the royal family:

- **You are a royal priest.** *But you are a chosen generation, a royal priesthood, a holy nation, His own special people.* (1 Peter 2:9, NKJV)

- **You are a king and a priest unto God.** *And has made us kings and priests unto God and his Father.* (Revelation 1:6)

- **You are a member of the family of God.** *For whom he did foreknow, he also did predestinate to be conformed to the image of his Son, that he might be the firstborn among many brethren.* (Romans 8:29) Paul says Christians, *"being many, are one body in Christ, and every one members one of another."* (Romans 12:5) Peter proclaims that we are *"a chosen generation, **a royal priesthood**, a holy nation, His own special people."* (1 Peter 2:9)

✦ **Your name is written in the Book of Life.** *"Rejoice, because your names are written in heaven."* (Luke 10:20)

Verbally stating our position in Christ is important: *"Let the redeemed of the Lord say so."* (Psalms 107:2) This reinforces and declares our position and authority. In Job 22:28, we are instructed to *"decree a thing, and it shall be established."* To decree is to issue a **royal** edict, with the legal authority of the crown. We have this right as royal priests!

4. A Pure Life.

✦ *He has showed you, O man, what is good; and what does the Lord require of you, but to do justly, and to love mercy, and to walk humbly with your God?* (Micah 6:8)

✦ *Then the Angel of the Lord spoke very solemnly to Joshua and said, "The Lord of Hosts declares: If you will follow the paths I set for you and do **all** I tell you to, then I will put you in charge of my Temple, to keep it holy; and I will let you walk in and out of my presence with these angels.* (Zechariah 3:7, The Living Bible) If Jesus is not Lord of everything, is he Lord of anything?

✦ *Wherefore putting away lying, speak every man truth with his neighbor: for we are members one of another. Be you angry, and sin not: let not the sun go down upon your wrath:* **Neither give place to the devil.** (Ephesians 4:25-27) These verses are telling us not to allow any specific point of entry into your life through ungodly conduct. The devil is trying to break in already. There is no need to invite him over.

. . . .

There is a story told of a man who was buying a house. In the course of negotiating the purchase, the seller asked for one concession: that he be allowed to retain one nail in the front door. The buyer saw no harm in this and agreed. But after receiving the money for the home, the previous owner hung a dead chicken on the nail, which soon began to smell. In fact, the odor became so repugnant that it affected the entire home, making it unbearable. Shortly, the new owner left. Satan only needs **one foothold** to create a horrible stench.
Don't let him have it.

. . . .

5. A Guarded Heart.

Proverbs 4:23 advises you to *"Keep your heart with all diligence; for out of it are the issues of life."* This means that there is a risk of your other endeavors supplanting God as your top priority. We all must be careful not to permit anyone or anything, other than God, to occupy the center of our lives. Satan would love to dilute your allegiance to God as he did with Judas, who allowed greed and betrayal into his heart, resulting in disaster: *"And supper being ended, the devil having now put into the heart of Judas Iscariot, Simon's son, to betray him."* (John 13:3) Is there anything you care about as much as God? Remove it, or God will.

6. Angels.

Hebrews 1:14 tells us that angels are *"all ministering spirits, sent forth to minister for them who shall be heirs of salvation?"* God sends them to help us. Matthew 18:10 tells us that every Christian has an angel. *"Take heed that you despise not one of these little ones; for I say unto you, That in heaven **their angels** do always behold the face of my Father which is in heaven."*

God dispatches angels **in response to our prayers**. An angel told Daniel, *"your request has been heard in heaven and was answered the very first day you began to fast before the Lord and pray for understanding; **that very day I was sent here to meet you.**"* (Daniel 10:12, TLB) In the early church, when Peter was thrown in prison, the Christians sent up prayer "without ceasing" and God sent an angel to free him. (Acts 12:5, 7)

*"Don't you realize that I could ask my Father for thousands of angels to protect us, and he would send them **instantly**?"* (Matthew 26:53, TLB) Ask God for the protection that only he can give: **angelic** protection.

7. God.

Ask God to rebuke the devil, as supported by Jude 1:9, Malachi 3:11, and Zechariah 3:1-2:

✦ *Yet Michael the archangel, when contending with the devil he disputed about the body of Moses, dared not bring against him a railing accusation, but **said, The Lord rebuke you.*** (Jude 1:9)

✦ *"And **I will rebuke the devourer** for your sakes, and he shall not destroy the fruits of your ground; neither shall your vine cast her fruit before the time in the field, says the Lord of hosts."* (Malachi 3:11)

✦ *And he showed me Joshua the high priest standing before the angel of the Lord, and Satan standing at his right hand to resist him. And the Lord said unto Satan, **The Lord rebuke you, O Satan**; even the Lord that has chosen Jerusalem rebuke you: is not this a brand plucked out of the fire?* (Zechariah 3:1-2)

✦ **Jesus is our Chief Shepherd and he is armed and very experienced in dealing with predators. Call upon him for protection.** *"Yes, though I walk through the valley of the shadow of death, **I will fear no evil**: for you are with me; **your rod and your staff they comfort me.**"* (Psalms 23:4).

Sample Lesson: Spiritual Warfare

8. Church Traditions.

The Apostle Paul, in Thessalonians 2:15, commands us to "stand fast, and **hold the traditions** which you have been taught, whether by word, or our epistle." For hundreds of years, Christians all over the world have recited the Apostles Creed as a declaration of our beliefs and standing in Christ.

I believe in God the Father Almighty, Maker of heaven and earth. And in Jesus Christ his only Son our Lord; who was conceived by the Holy Ghost, born of the Virgin Mary, suffered under Pontius Pilate, was crucified, dead, and buried; he descended into hell; the third day he rose again from the dead; he ascended into heaven, and sits on the right hand of God the Father Almighty; from there he shall come to judge the quick and the dead. I believe in the Holy Ghost; the holy catholic Church; the communion of saints; the forgiveness of sins; the resurrection of the body; and the life everlasting. AMEN.

....

Resist *the devil, and he will flee from you.* (James 4:7)

Part 4: DEED

✦ Are you about to start a project which you want to protect from Satan?

✦ How can you prevent the devil's interference?

✦ Do you feel confident about confronting the enemy? Why?

✦ Kick the devil out of your work, verbally, in the name of Jesus.

✦ Keep him out by commanding him not to return or retaliate.

✦ Then, ask God to bless your endeavors.

Chapter 24

Sample Lesson: Prayer

Part 1: SEED

… one of his disciples said unto him, Lord, teach us to pray….

"When you pray, say …"
Our Father which art in heaven, Hallowed be thy name. Thy kingdom come. Thy will be done, as in heaven, so in earth. Give us day by day our daily bread. And forgive us our sins; for we also forgive every one that is indebted to us. And lead us not into temptation; but deliver us from evil.
(Luke, Chapter 11)

In the Lord's Prayer, Jesus taught us to offer:

1. **Exaltation**: Approach God with love and honor. *"Our Father which art in heaven, Hallowed by thy name."*
2. **Recognition**: Submit to his will and Lordship. *"Thy kingdom come. Thy will be done."*
3. **Petition**: Ask him to meet our needs. *"Give us day by day our daily bread."*
4. **Confession**: Ask forgiveness and state our forgiveness of others. *"And forgive us our sins; for we also forgive everyone that is indebted to us."*
5. **Obedience**: Ask for guidance away from sin, evil, and the devil. *"And lead us not into temptation; but deliver us from evil."*

What prayer is <u>NOT</u>:

1. Prayer is <u>not</u> informing God of things he does not know.

✦ *"You know what I am going to say before I even say it."* (Psalm 139:4, The Living Bible)

✦ *"Remember, your Father knows exactly what you need even before you ask him!"* (Matthew 6:8, The Living Bible)

2. Prayer is <u>not</u> about getting God's attention.

✦ *"You both precede and follow me, and place your hand of blessing on my head."* (Psalm 139:5, TLB)

✦ *"According as he has chosen us in him before the foundation of the world."* (Ephesians 1:4)

✦ *"You saw me before I was born and scheduled each day of my life before I began to breathe. Every day was recorded in your Book!"* (Psalm 139:16, TLB)

3. Prayer is *not* repeating a liturgical stanza over and over.

"But when you pray, use not vain repetitions, as the heathen do: for they think that they shall be heard for their much speaking." (Matthew 6:7)

4. Prayer is *not* a last resort.

✦ *But I cry to you for help, Lord, in the morning my prayer comes before you."* (Psalm 88:13 NIV)

✦ *But I will sing of your power; yes, I will sing aloud of your mercy in the morning.* (Psalms 59:16)

5. Prayer is *not* just for special occasions.

✦ *Now when Daniel knew that the writing was signed, he went into his house; and his windows being open in his chamber toward Jerusalem,* **he kneeled upon his knees three times a day***, and prayed, and gave thanks before his God, as he did aforetime.* (Daniel 6:10)

✦ ***Evening, and morning, and at noon, will I pray****, and cry aloud: and he shall hear my voice.* (Psalms 55:17)

✦ *Rejoice evermore. Pray without ceasing.* ***In everything*** *give thanks: for this is the will of God in Christ Jesus concerning you.* (1 Thessalonians 5:16-18)

Sample Lesson: Prayer

Part 2: NEED
Benefits of prayer.

At our seaport, there is a man who works high above the pier in the control cabin of a crane. He loads and unloads ships by operating levers to bring the strength of the crane over heavy cargo containers. Much like those levers move the powerful arm of the crane, **prayer** moves the mighty arm of the Lord. **You** can move the hand of God.
*Thus says the Lord, the Holy One of Israel, and his Maker, Ask me of things to come concerning my sons, and concerning the work of my hands **command you me**. (Isaiah 45:11)*

Why should we pray? Through prayer, you:

1. Obtain anything you ask.
✦ *Again I say unto you, That if two of you shall agree on earth as touching any thing that they shall ask, it shall be done for them of my Father which is in heaven. (Matthew 18:19)*
✦ *And whatsoever you shall ask in my name, that will I do, that the Father may be glorified in the Son. If you shall ask any thing in my name, I will do it. (John 14:13-14)*
✦ *And this is the confidence that we have in him, that, if we ask any thing according to his will, he hears us: And if we know that he hear us, whatsoever we ask, we know that we have the petitions that we desired of him. (1 John 5:14-15)*

2. Please God by exercising your faith.
✦ *But without faith it is impossible to please him: for he that comes to God must believe that he is, and that he is a rewarder of them that diligently seek him. (Hebrews 11:6)*
✦ *But let him ask in faith, nothing wavering. (James 1:6)*

3. Approach God by giving thanks.
✦ *Be thankful. (Colossions 3:15)*
✦ *Enter into his gates with thanksgiving, and into his courts with praise: be thankful unto him, and bless his name. (Psalms 100:4)*

4. Avoid ignorance.
✦ *Because that, when they knew God, they glorified him not as God, neither were thankful; but became vain in their imaginations, and their foolish heart was darkened. Professing themselves to be wise, **they became fools.** (Romans 1:21-22)*
✦ *Call to Me, and I will answer you, and show you great and mighty things, which you do not know. (Jeremiah 33:1, NKJV)*

5. Commune with God.
But you are holy, O you that inhabits the praises of Israel. (Psalm 22:3)

6. Accomplish great things through faith.
The effectual fervent prayer of a righteous man avails much. (James 5:16)

7. Obtain physical healing and forgiveness.
Is any sick among you? let him call for the elders of the church; and let them pray over him, anointing him with oil in the name of the Lord: And the prayer of faith shall save the sick, and the Lord shall raise him up; and if he has committed sins, they shall be forgiven him. (James 5:14-15)

8. Receive wise guidance.
If you want to know what God wants you to do, ask him, and he will gladly tell you, for he is always ready to give a bountiful supply of wisdom to all who ask him; he will not resent it. (James 1:5, TLB)

9. Receive angelic assistance.
Peter therefore was kept in prison: **but prayer was made without ceasing** *of the church unto God for him. And when Herod would have brought him forth, the same night Peter was sleeping between two soldiers, bound with two chains: and the keepers before the door kept the prison. And,* **behold, the angel of the Lord came upon him***, and a light shined in the prison: and he smote Peter on the side, and raised him up, saying, Arise up quickly. And his chains fell off from his hands.* (Acts 12:5)

10. Receive strength for spiritual warfare.
Howbeit this kind goes not out but by prayer and fasting. (Matthew 17:21)

11. Receive the peace of God.
Be anxious for nothing, but in everything by prayer and supplication, with thanksgiving, let your requests be made known to God; and the **peace of God***, which surpasses all understanding, will guard your hearts and minds through Christ Jesus.* (Philippians 4:6-7)

12. Receive strength to minister.
✦ *These all continued with one accord in prayer and supplication, with the women, and Mary the mother of Jesus, and with his brethren. And in those days Peter stood up in the midst of the disciples, and said ...* (Acts 1:14-15)
✦ *But we will give ourselves continually to prayer, and to the ministry of the word.* (Acts 6:4)

13. Receive the Holy Spirit.
If you then, being evil, know how to give good gifts unto your children: how much more shall your heavenly Father give the Holy Spirit **to them that ask him***?* (Luke 11:13)

14. Help others.
For I know that this will turn out for my deliverance **through your prayer** *...*
(Philippians 1:19, NKJV)

15. Receive guidance.
Thus says the Lord, the Holy One of Israel, and his Maker, Ask me of things to come concerning my sons, and concerning the work of my hands command me. (Isaiah 45:11)

16. Receive opportunities to preach.
Don't forget to pray for us too, that God will give us many chances to preach the Good News of Christ. (Colossians 4:3, TLB)

....

Discussion Question:
How do you know when you have "prayed through" a situation and received an answer?

....

What are the consequences of *not* praying?

1. Unsatisfied needs:
Where do wars and fights come from among you? Do they not come from your desires for pleasure that war in your members? You lust and do not have. You murder and covet and cannot obtain. You fight and war. **Yet you do not have because you do not ask.** (James 4:2)

2. Ineffectiveness:
John Wesley said *"God does nothing, except by prayer."*

3. Sin against the Lord:
Moreover, as for me, far be it from me that I should sin against the Lord in ceasing to pray for you. (1 Samuel 12:23, NKJV)

4. Lack of power.
If you pray a little, you get a little power. If you pray a lot, you get a lot of power.

5. Anxiety:
Get rid of those burdens: *"Casting all your care upon him; for he cares for you."* (1 Peter 5:7).

6. Punishment:
And them that are turned back from the Lord; and those that have not sought the Lord, **nor inquired for him**....*Hold your peace at the presence of the Lord God: for the day of the Lord is at hand: for the Lord has prepared a sacrifice, he has bid his guests. And it shall come to pass in the day of the Lord's sacrifice, that* **I will punish** ... (Zephaniah 1:6-8)

Have you ever bought a home or a car without praying about it? Did you learn anything?

Part 3: FEED
What the Bible says about prayer.

What qualities does a person of prayer possess?

- **Seeks God's priorities first.** *But seek ye first the kingdom of God, and his righteousness; and all these things shall be added unto you.* (Matthew 6:33)
- **Is shameless in his persistence.** *Suppose you went to a friend's house at midnight, wanting to borrow three loaves of bread. You would shout up to him, 'A friend of mine has just arrived for a visit and I've nothing to give him to eat.' He would call down from his bedroom, 'Please don't ask me to get up. The door is locked for the night and we are all in bed. I just can't help you this time.' "But I'll tell you this – though he won't do it as a friend, **if you keep knocking long enough** he will get up and give you everything you want – just because of your persistence (shamelessness)."* (Luke 11:5-8) Here, Jesus tells the story of someone who was not afraid to be embarrassed. He **"prayed through"** until he got his answer. He was desperate, but this turned out to be an asset. He refused to quit.
- **Hungers to be in the presence of God.**
  - *I long, yes, faint with longing to be able to enter your courtyard and come near to the Living God.* (Psalm 84:2, TLB)
  - *As the deer pants for water, so I long for you, O God. I thirst for God, the living God.* (Psalms 42:1, NKJV)
- **May have sorrow.**
  - ***Out of the abundance of my complaint and grief have I spoken hitherto.*** *Then Eli answered and said, Go in peace: and the God of Israel grant you your petition that you have asked of him.* (1 Samuel 1:15-17)
  - *The children of Israel sighed by reason of the bondage, and they cried, and their cry came up unto God by reason of the bondage.* ***And God heard their groaning.*** (Exodus 2:23-24)
- **Understands that all blessings come from God.** *Every good gift and every perfect gift is from above, and comes down from the Father of lights.* (James 1:17)
- **Knows that only God can help.**
  - *He **only** is my rock and my salvation; he is my defense; I shall not be greatly moved.*
  - *My soul, wait thou only upon God; for my expectation is from him.*
  - *He **only** is my rock and my salvation.* (Psalms 62:2, 5, 6)
- **Knows that the Lord treasures prayer.** *And when he had taken the book, the four beasts and four and twenty elders fell down before the Lamb, having everyone of them harps, and golden vials full of odors, which are **the prayers of saints**.* (Revelation 5:8, TLB)
- **Knows God longs to be generous to us.** *Yet the Lord longs to be gracious to you; he rises to show you compassion. For the Lord is a God of justice. Blessed are all who wait for Him!* (Isaiah 30:18)
- **Knows that sometimes the answers to prayer take time to arrive.** *Then said he unto me, Fear not, Daniel: for from the first day that you did set your heart to understand, and to chasten yourself before your God, your words were heard, and I am come for your words. But the prince of the kingdom of Persia withstood me one and twenty days: but, lo, Michael, one of the chief princes, came to help me; and I remained there with the kings of Persia.* ***Now I am come … When you wait on God, it shows you have faith that he will answer.***
- **Knows that we need to be ready to pray in an instant.** *Rejoicing in hope; patient in tribulation; continuing instant in prayer.* (Romans 12:12)

- ✦ **Knows that we need to believe when we pray.**
  And all things, whatsoever you shall ask in prayer, believing, you shall receive. (Matthew 21:22)
- ✦ **Knows the unlimited power of faith. All that's required is that you really believe and have no doubt!** *Listen to me! You can pray for anything, and if you believe, you have it; it's yours!* (Mark 11:23, 24, TLB)

What things hinder prayer?

- ✦ **Unforgiveness.** *But when you are praying, **first forgive** anyone you are holding a grudge against, so that your Father in heaven will forgive you your sins too.* (Mark 11:25, TLB)
- ✦ **Unkindness.** *Likewise, ye husbands, dwell with them according to knowledge, giving honor unto the wife, as unto the weaker vessel, and as being heirs together of the grace of life; that your prayers be not hindered.* (I Peter 3:7)
- ✦ **Unbelief.** *But let him ask in faith, with no doubting, for he who doubts is like a wave of the sea driven and tossed by the wind.* **For let not that man suppose that he will receive anything from the Lord.** (James 1:6-7)
- ✦ **Unthankfulness.** *As they were increased, so they sinned against me: therefore will I change their glory into shame.* (Hosea 4:7)
- ✦ **Unconcern for others.** *You ask and do not receive, because you ask amiss, that you may spend it on your pleasures.* (James 4:3)
- ✦ **Unconcealed prayer.** *But you, when you pray, enter into your closet, and when you have shut your door, pray to your Father which is in secret; and your Father which sees **in secret** shall reward you openly.* (Matthew 6:6)
- ✦ **Unconfessed sin.** *If I regard iniquity in my heart, the Lord will **not** hear me.* (Psalms 66:18)

How to Pray

- ✦ **EXALTATION.** Our Father in heaven, hallowed be Your name.
  - We approach God with boldness because he is our Father, but also with utmost sacred reverence because he is our Creator and Ruler. God dwells in our praise. Praise is the way to enter into God's presence.
    - But you are holy, O you that inhabits the praises of Israel. (Psalm 22:3)
- ✦ **RECOGNITION OF GOD's SOVEREIGNTY.** Your kingdom come. Your will be done on earth as it is in heaven. Prayer is no time to be puffed up.
  - Submit yourselves therefore to God. (James 4:7)
  - "…he forgets not the cry of the humble." (Psalm 9:12)
  - Humble yourselves in the sight of the Lord, and he shall lift you up. (James 4:10)
- ✦ **PETITION.** Give us this day our daily bread. **Inch by inch, life's a cinch.**
  - So don't be anxious about tomorrow. God will take care of your tomorrow too. Live one day at a time. (Matthew 6:34, TLB)
- ✦ **CONFESSION.**
  - And forgive us our sins, for we also forgive everyone who is indebted to us.
  - And whenever you stand praying, if you have anything against anyone, forgive him, that your Father in heaven may also forgive you your trespasses. But if you do not forgive, neither will your Father in heaven forgive your trespasses. (Mark 11:26)
- ✦ **OBEDIENCE.** And lead us not into temptation, but deliver us from the evil one.
  - Search me, O God, and know my heart: try me, and know my thoughts: And see if there be any wicked way in me, and lead me in the way everlasting. (Psalm 139:23-24)

Why Does God Answer Our Prayers?

1. **Because He is your good Father.**
   a. *God, who richly supplies us with all things to enjoy. (1 Timothy 6:17) NASB)*
   b. *He who did not spare His own Son, but delivered Him over for us all, how will He not also with Him freely give us all things? (Romans 8:32, NASB)*
   c. *For God so loved the world, that he gave his only Son, that whoever believes in him should not perish but have eternal life. (John 3:16, ESV)*
   d. *If you then, being evil, know how to give good gifts to your children, how much more will your Father who is in heaven give good things to those who ask Him! (Matthew 7:11, NKJV)*
2. **Because Jesus is your Brother and He lives to intercede for you.**
   a. *He always lives to intercede for them. (Hebrews 7:25, NIV)*
   b. *I do not pray for these alone, but also for those who will believe in Me through their word. (John 17:20-21)*
3. **When God answers your prayers, it brings Him glory and honor.**
   a. *When you produce much fruit, you are my true disciples. This brings great glory to my Father. (John 15:8, NLT)*
   b. *And whatever you ask in My name, that I will do, that the Father may be glorified in the Son. If you ask anything in My name, I will do it. (John 14:13, NKJV)*
4. **God enjoys providing for you.**
   a. *Yes, let them say continually, Let the LORD be magnified, which has pleasure in the prosperity of his servant. (Psalm 35:27)*
   b. *For the LORD takes pleasure in His people. (Psalm 149:4, NKJV)*
5. **To keep you from sinning.**
   a. *Get up and pray, so that you will not give in to temptation. (Luke 22:46, NLT)*
   b. *And the Lord said, Simon, Simon, behold, Satan has desired to have you, that he may sift you as wheat: but I have prayed for you, that your faith fail not. (Luke 22:31-32)*
6. **To make you productive in evangelism.**
   a. *Yes, I am the vine; you are the branches. Those who remain in me, and I in them, will produce much fruit. For apart from me you can do nothing. (John 15:5, NLT)*
   b. *Therefore pray the Lord of the harvest to send out laborers into His harvest. (Matthew 9:38, NKJV)*
7. **To control governments and nations, so that we can live peacefully.**
   a. *Therefore I exhort first of all that supplications, prayers, intercessions, and giving of thanks be made for all men, for kings and all who are in authority, that we may lead a quiet and peaceable life in all godliness and reverence. For this is good and acceptable in the sight of God our Savior. (1 Timothy 2:1-3, NKJV)*
   b. *Just as water is turned into irrigation ditches, so the Lord directs the king's thoughts. He turns them wherever he wants to. (Proverbs 21:1, TLB)*
8. **To accomplish His will on earth.**
   a. *Your kingdom come. Your will be done on earth as it is in heaven. (Matthew 6:10, NKJV)*
9. **To take care of us; to provide our daily needs.**
   a. *And my God shall supply all your need according to His riches in glory by Christ Jesus. (Philippians 4:19, NKJV)*
   b. *Know that the LORD, He is God; It is He who has made us, and not we ourselves; We are His people and the sheep of His pasture. (Psalm 100:3, NKJV)*
   c. *Give us this day our daily bread. (Matthew 6:11, NKJV)*

Sample Lesson: Prayer

10. **To cleanse us and make us acceptable to Him.**
    a. *But your iniquities have separated you from your God; and your sins have hidden His face from you, so that He will not hear. (Isaiah 59;2, NKJV).*
    b. *Let us therefore come boldly to the throne of grace, that we may obtain mercy and find grace to help in time of need. (Hebrews 4:16).*
11. **To protect His great reputation and name.**
    a. *Nevertheless he saved them for his name's sake, that he might make his mighty power to be known. (Psalm 106:8)*
    b. *For the glory of your name, O LORD, preserve my life. Because of your faithfulness, bring me out of this distress. (Psalm 143:11, NLT)*
12. **To make us like His Son, Jesus Christ.**
    a. *He went a little farther and fell on His face, and prayed. (Matthew 26:39, NKJV)*
    b. *I pray for them. I do not pray for the world but for those whom You have given Me, for they are Yours. (John 17:9, NKJV)*
13. **To enlighten us.**
    a. *Call unto me, and I will answer you, and show you great and mighty things, which you know not. (Jeremiah 33:3)*
    b. *If you need wisdom, ask our generous God, and he will give it to you. (James 1:5, NLT)*
14. **To help us because he cares for us.**
    a. *He cares for us. (1 Peter 5:7)*
    b. *Cast your burden upon the LORD, and he shall sustain you: he shall never suffer the righteous to be moved. (Psalm 55:22, KJV)*
    c. *How often would I have gathered your children together, even as a hen gathers her chickens under her wings. (Matthew 23:37)*
15. **Because you and God are dear friends.**
    a. *And the LORD spoke unto Moses face to face, as a man speaks unto his friend.* (Exodus 33:11)
    b. *Jesus wept. Then said the Jews, Behold how he loved him! (John 11:35-36).*
    c. *Then the disciple whom Jesus loved leaned back against Jesus' chest and asked him. (John 13:25, NET).*

Part 4: DEED
Apply. Pray for opportunities to pray!

✦ List any obstacles to prayer in your life and the corrective action required.

✦ List five people you will pray for this week.

✦ Fast one meal and pray for someone you love.

✦ Like Daniel, keep appointments with God in the morning, at noon, and at evening.

✦ Start a prayer journal to record prayers and God's answers.

✦ Don't forget to thank God for his answers.

✦ Remember the acronym **"PUSH."** (Pray Until Something Happens).

Chapter 25

Sample Lesson: Teamwork

Part 1: SEED

Biblical teamwork: One body, many members.

For as the body is one and has many members, but all the members of that one body, being many, are one body, so also is Christ. For by one Spirit we were all baptized into one body – whether Jews or Greeks, whether slaves or free – and have all been made to drink into one Spirit. For in fact the body is not one member but many. If the foot should say, "Because I am not a hand, I am not of the body," is it therefore not of the body? And if the ear should say, "Because I am not of the eye, I am not of the body," is it therefore not of the body?
If the whole body were an eye, where would be the hearing? *If the whole were hearing, where would be the smelling? But now God has set the members, each one of them, in the body just as He pleased. And if they were all one member, where would the body be? But now there are many members, yet one body. And the eye cannot say to the hand, "I have no need of you;" nor again the head to the feet, "I have no need of you."*
(1 Corinthians 12:12-21, NKJV)

✦ **Teams are different from groups because the members:**
- Work together as God leads.
- Need one another to function well.
- Have different gifts to offer to the team.

✦ **Each and every team member has a unique and valuable contribution to make. These contributions are physical, mental, emotional, and spiritual.**
- *But each one has his own gift from God.* (1 Corinthians 7:7, NKJV)
- *God has given each of you some special abilities; be sure to use them to help each other.* (1 Peter 4:10, The Living Bible)

✦ **Team members share in victory and defeat.**
- *If one part suffers, all parts suffer with it, and if one part is honored, all the parts are glad.* (1 Corinthians 12:26, TLB)
- *For we are members one of another.* (Ephesians 4:25)
- *Bear one another's burdens, and so fulfill the law of Christ.* (Paul, in Galatians 6:2)
- *Let each of you look out not only for his own interests, but also for the interests of others.* (Philippians 2:4 NKJV)
- *Rejoice with them that do rejoice, and weep with them that weep.* (Romans 12:15)

Part 2: NEED
Why do we need teams?

1. To Accomplish Great Things without Burn-out. (Exodus 18:13-27)

✦ *And it came to pass on the morrow, that Moses sat to judge the people: and the people stood by Moses from the morning unto the evening. And when Moses' father in law saw all that he did to the people, he said, What is this thing that you do to the people?* **Why sit yourself alone, and all the people stand by you from morning unto evening?** *And Moses said unto his father in law, because the people come unto me to inquire of God: When they have a matter, they come unto me; and I judge between one and another, and I do make them know the statutes of God, and his laws. And Moses' father in law said unto him,* **The thing that you do is not good.** *You will surely wear away, both you, and this people that is with you: for this thing is too heavy for you; you are not able to perform it yourself alone. Hearken now unto my voice, I will give you counsel, and* **God shall be with you:** *be for the people to God-ward, that you may bring the causes unto God: And you shall teach them ordinances and laws, and shall show them the way wherein they must walk, and the work that they must do. Moreover you shall provide out of all the people* **able men, such as fear God,** *men of truth, hating covetousness; and place such over them, to be rulers of thousands, and rulers of hundreds, rulers of fifties, and rulers of tens: And let them judge the people at all seasons: and it shall be, that every great matter they shall bring unto you, but every small matter they shall judge: so shall it be easier for yourself, and they shall bear the burden with you. If you shall do this thing, and God commands you so, then you shalt be able to endure, and all this people shall also go to their place in peace. So Moses hearkened to the voice of his father in law, and did all that he had said. And Moses chose able men out of all Israel, and made them heads over the people, rulers of thousands, rulers of hundreds, rulers of fifties, and rulers of tens. And they judged the people at all seasons: the hard causes they brought unto Moses, but every small matter they judged themselves.*

2. To Provide Safety

✦ *Two are better than one, because they have a good reward for their labor. For if they fall, one will lift up his companion. But woe to him who is alone when he falls, for he has no one to help him up. Again, if two lie down together, they will keep warm; but how can one be warm alone?* **Though one may be overpowered by another, two can withstand him. And a threefold cord is not quickly broken.** (King Solomon, in Ecclesiastes 4:9-12, NKJV)

✦ *In a multitude of people is a king's honor, But in the lack of people is the downfall of the prince.* (Proverbs 14:28)

3. To Ensure Accountability

✦ *Then the disciples, every man according to his ability, determined to send relief unto the brethren which dwelt in Judaea: Which also they did, and sent it to the elders* **by the hands of Barnabas and Saul.** *(Acts 11:28-30)*

✦ *Let the righteous smite me; it shall be a kindness: and let him reprove me; it shall be an excellent oil...* (Psalms 141:5)

✦ *Open rebuke is better than secret love. Faithful are the wounds of a friend ...* (Proverbs 27:5, 6)

4. To Achieve through the Power of Unity (Genesis 11: 1-6)

And the whole earth was of **one language, and of one speech.** *And it came to pass, as they journeyed from the east, that they found a plain in the land of Shinar; and they dwelt there. And they said one to another, Go to, let us make brick, and burn them thoroughly. And they had brick for stone, and slime had they for mortar. And they said, Go to, let us build us a city and a tower, whose top may reach unto heaven; and let us make us a name, lest we be scattered abroad upon the face of the whole earth. And the Lord came down to see the city and the tower, which the children of men built. And the Lord said, Behold the people is one, and they have all one language; and this they begin to do: and* **now nothing will be restrained from them,** *which they have imagined to do.*

5. To Receive God's Blessings because of Unity

Psalms 133. **Behold**, *how good and how pleasant it is for brethren to dwell together* **in unity**! *It is like the precious ointment upon the head, that ran down upon the beard, even Aaron's beard: that went down to the skirts of his garments; As the dew of Hermon, and as the dew that descended upon the mountains of Zion: for* **there the Lord commanded the blessing,** *even life for evermore.*

6. To Provide a Testimony

✦ *By this shall all men know that you are my disciples, if you have love one to another.* (Jesus, in John 13:35)

✦ *Of Zebulun, such as went forth to battle,* **expert** *in war, with all instruments of war, fifty thousand,* **which could keep rank**: *they were not of double heart.* (1 Chronicles 12:33).

✦ *Behold, how good and how pleasant it is for brethren to dwell together in* **unity**! (Psalms 133:1)

Part 3: FEED

1. The One Team Member you *must* have for success.

✦ *Take care to live in me, and let me live in you.* **For a branch can't produce fruit when severed from the vine** *(apart from Jesus). Nor can you be fruitful apart from me.*
(John 15:4)

✦ *Am I a God at hand, said the Lord, and not a God afar off?* (Jeremiah 23:23)

✦ *Draw nigh to God, and he will draw nigh to you.* (James 4:8)

✦ *For where two or three are gathered together* **in my name,** *there am I in the midst of them.*
(Matthew 18:20)

2. The Team Leader Should not be Worshipped

✦ *Who then is Paul, and who is Apollos, but ministers (helpers) by whom you believed,* **even as the Lord gave to every man**?

✦ *I have planted, Apollos watered; but God gave the increase. So then neither is he that plants any thing, neither he that waters; but God that gives the increase. Now he that plants and he that waters are one: and every man shall receive his own reward according to his own labor. For we are laborers together with God ...* (1 Corinthians 3:6-9)

✦ *Our attitude should be that of John the Baptist, who stated,* "*He must increase, but I must decrease.*" (John 3:30)

When you let the Lord on-board, you accomplish your goals.
✦ *And when they (Jesus and Peter) were come into the ship, the wind ceased.*
(Matthew 14:32)

✦ *But he said unto them, It is I; be not afraid. Then they willingly received him into the ship: and* **immediately the ship was at the land** *whither they went.* (John 6:20, 21)

3. Your Team's Success Depends on God. (David, in 2 Samuel 22:22-25)

✦ *For I have kept the ways of the Lord, and have not wickedly departed from my God. For all his judgments were before me: and as for his statutes, I did not depart from them. I was also upright before him, and have kept myself from mine iniquity.*

✦ *Therefore the Lord has recompensed me* **according to my righteousness;** *according to my cleanness in his eyesight.*

Sample Lesson: Teamwork

What if David had been unrighteous? How would the Lord have recompensed him?

✦ **Leviticus 26:3-8**
   If you walk in my statutes, and keep my commandments, and do them;
   Then *I will give you rain in due season, and the land shall yield her increase, and the trees of the field shall yield their fruit.*
   And your threshing shall reach unto the vintage, and the vintage shall reach unto the sowing time: and you shall eat your bread to the full, and dwell in your land safely.
   And I will give peace in the land, and you shall lie down, and none shall make you afraid: and I will rid evil beasts out of the land, neither shall the sword go through your land.
   And you shall chase your enemies, and they shall fall before you by the sword.
   And five of you shall chase a hundred*, and a hundred of you shall put ten thousand to flight: and your enemies shall fall before you by the sword.*

✦ **Proverbs 16:7**
   When a man's ways please the Lord, he makes even his enemies to be at peace with him.

✦ **Psalms 127:1, 2**
   Except the Lord build the house (the team), they labor in vain that build it: except the Lord keep the city, the watchman wakes but in vain.
   It is vain for you to rise up early, to sit up late, to eat the bread of sorrows: for so he gives his beloved sleep.

4. But, You Need to Know that ... *It is a fearful thing to fall into the hands of the living God.* (Hebrews 10:31)

Remember what happened when David pridefully took a census: thousands of his army died. If anything gets between you and God, he will destroy it.

✦ **If you depart from God, He will scatter your team.** *But if you will not hearken unto me, and will not do all these commandments; And if you shall despise my statutes, or if your soul abhor my judgments, so that you will not do all my commandments, but that you break my covenant: I also will do this unto you; I will even appoint over you terror, consumption, and the burning ague, that shall consume the eyes, and cause sorrow of heart: and you shall sow your seed in vain, for your enemies shall eat it. And I will set my face against you, and you shall be slain before your enemies: they that hate you shall reign over you; and you shall flee when none pursues you.* **And I will scatter you among the heathen,** *and will draw out a sword after you: and your land shall be desolate, and your cities waste. Then shall the land enjoy her sabbaths, as long as it lies desolate, and you be in your enemies' land; even then shall the land rest, and enjoy her sabbaths. As long as it lies desolate it shall rest; because it did not rest in your sabbaths, when you dwelled upon it.* (Leviticus 26:14-35)

✦ *For, lo, they that are far from you shall perish: you have destroyed all them that go a whoring from you.* (Psalms 73:27)

✦ *Work hard and cheerfully at all you do, just as though you were working for the Lord and not merely for your masters, remembering that it is the Lord Christ who is going to pay you, giving you your full portion of all he owns. He is the one you are really working for.* **And if you don't do your best for him, he will pay you in a way that you won't like ...**
(Colossians 3:23-25, The Living Bible)

Sample Lesson: Teamwork

Part 4: DEED

Are you (still) on God's team?
Deuteronomy 32: 29-30 The Living Bible

Oh, that they were wise! Oh, that they could understand!
Oh, that they would know what they are getting into!
How could one single enemy chase a thousand of them,
And two put ten thousand to flight,
Unless their Rock had abandoned them,
Unless the Lord had destroyed them?

Chapter 26

Sample Lesson: Suffering

Since Christ suffered and underwent pain, you must have the same attitude he did; you must be ready to suffer, too. (1 Peter 4:1)

Part 1: SEED

What do Peter, Paul, John, and Jesus have in common? *Suffering.*
All underwent criticism and physical suffering as they carried out their good work on earth. If you live a godly life, you will also experience pain. The Bible tells us that *"**all** that will live godly in Christ Jesus shall suffer persecution."* (2 Timothy 3:12) The following are some examples of the persecution and suffering described in the Bible:

✦ Temptation. (Hebrews 2:18)

✦ Reproach or the discrediting of character. (1 Peter 4:14 and Luke 6:22)

✦ Imprisonment and whipping. (Acts 16:23)

✦ Insults and physical abuse. (John 19:3)

✦ Pursuit into hiding. (John 20:19)

✦ Beating. (2 Corinthians 11:24)

✦ Stoning. (2 Corinthians 11:25 and Acts, Chapter 7)

✦ Perils in travel, including robbers. (2 Corinthians 11:26)

✦ Fatigue, hunger, thirst, cold, and lack of clothing. (2 Corinthians 11:24)

✦ Loss of possessions. (Philippians 3:8)

✦ Hatred. (Luke 6:22)

✦ Separation from others. (Luke 6:22)

✦ Betrayal. (Matthew 26:2)

✦ Crucifixion. (Matthew 26:2)

Part 2: NEED

Should you expect to suffer?

✦ *It is enough for the disciple that he be as his master, and the servant as his lord. If they have called the master of the house Beelzebub, **how much more shall they call them of his household**?* (Matthew 10:25)

✦ *But Jesus answered and said, You know not what you ask. Are you able to drink of the cup that I shall drink of, and to be baptized with the baptism that I am baptized with? They say unto him, We are able. And he said unto them, **You shall drink indeed of my cup.*** (Matthew 20:22-23)

✦ *There is no man that has left house, or brethren, or sisters, or father, or mother, or wife, or children, or lands, for my sake, and the gospel's, but he shall receive a hundredfold now in this time, houses, and brethren, and sisters, and mothers, and children, and lands, with persecutions; and in the world to come eternal life.* (Mark 10:28-30)

Why do we suffer?

✦ **Suffering identifies us with Christ now and in his glory to come.** In other words, our suffering for Christ is evidence that we will receive the same inheritance (glory) as one of God's Children and reign with him one day.

- *The Spirit itself bears witness with our spirit, that we are the children of God: And if children, then heirs; heirs of God, and joint-heirs with Christ; if so be that we suffer with him, that we may be also glorified together. For I reckon that the sufferings of this present time are not worthy to be compared with the glory which shall be revealed in us.* (Romans 8:16-18)
- *It is a faithful saying: For if we be dead with him, we shall also live with him: if we suffer, we shall also reign with him: if we deny him, he also will deny us.* (2 Timothy 2:11-12)

✦ **By suffering, we follow Christ's example.** *For even hereunto were you called: because Christ also suffered for us, leaving us an example, that you should follow his steps.* (1 Peter 2:21)

✦ **We conquer the flesh through suffering.** *For remember, when your body suffers, sin loses its power, and you won't be spending the rest of your life chasing after evil desires, but will be anxious to do the will of God.* (1 Peter 4:1b-2)

✦ **We become like Christ through suffering.** *And be found in him, not having mine own righteousness, which is of the law, but that which is through the faith of Christ, the righteousness which is of God by faith: That I may know him, and the power of his resurrection, and the fellowship of his sufferings, being made conformable unto his death.* (Philippians 3:9-10)

When a refiner is purifying gold he passes it over the fire several times. Each time brings dross to the surface, which he removes. Finally, when the gold is so pure that he can see his own image, he molds the gold into a beautiful instrument. Proverbs 12:6 tells us: *The words of the Lord are pure words: as silver tried in a furnace of earth, purified **seven times**.*
Fiery trials make us more and more like Jesus.

- **To receive a blessing when we have been faithful.** *Blessed is the man that endures temptation: for when he is tried, he shall receive **the crown of life**, which the Lord has promised to them that love him.* (James 1:12)

- **For God to point out our faithfulness in the spirit world.** *And the Lord said unto Satan, Have you considered my servant Job, that there is none like him in the earth, a perfect and an upright man, one that fears God, and eschews evil?* (Job 1:8)

- **To have fellowship with Jesus.** *That I may know him, and the power of his resurrection, and the fellowship of his sufferings, being made conformable unto his death; if by any means I might attain unto the resurrection of the dead.* (Philippians 3:10-11)

- **To honor Christ.** *For whom he did foreknow, he also did predestinate to be conformed to the image of his Son, that he might be the firstborn among many brethren.* (Romans 8:29)

- **To remain humble.** *And lest I (Paul) should be exalted above measure through the abundance of the revelations, there was given to me a thorn in the flesh, the messenger of Satan to buffet me, lest I should be exalted above measure.* (2 Corinthians 12:7)

- **To receive and to rely on Christ's strength.** *For this thing I besought the Lord thrice, that it might depart from me. And he said unto me, My grace is sufficient for you: for my strength is made perfect in weakness. Most gladly therefore will I rather glory in my infirmities, that the power of Christ may rest upon me.* (2 Corinthians 12:8-9)

- **To increase our faith and be counted "worthy of the kingdom of God."** *He is using your sufferings to make you ready for his kingdom, while at the same time he is preparing judgment and punishment for those who are hurting you.* (2 Thessalonians 1:5)

- **To build our spiritual might.**
  - *Here is a list of the nations the Lord left in the land to test the new generation of Israel who had not experienced the wars of Canaan. For God wanted to give opportunity to the youth of Israel to exercise faith and obedience in conquering their enemies.* (Judges 3:1-2)
  - *And when the devil had ended all the temptation, he departed from him for a season. And Jesus returned in the power of the Spirit into Galilee …* (Luke 4:13-14)
  - *Can you think of someone in the Bible who failed the test of temptation and lost his strength?* (Samson)

- **To increase our patience.** *And not only so, but we glory in tribulations also: knowing that tribulation works patience.* (Romans 5:3)

- ✦ **To prosper us.** *But the more they afflicted them, the more they multiplied and grew.* (Exodus 1:12)

- ✦ **To please God.** *Of course, you get no credit for being patient if you are beaten for doing wrong; but if you do right and suffer for it, and are patient beneath the blows, God is well pleased.* (1 Peter 2:20, TLB)

- ✦ **To enable us to comfort others.** *When others are troubled, needing our sympathy and encouragement, we can pass on to them this same help and comfort God has given us.* (2 Corinthians 1:4)

....

One time a little boy found a cocoon. He felt sorry for the butterfly inside that was trying to free itself, so he decided to open the cocoon. However, when he did, he noticed that the butterfly was unable to fly because its wings had not fully developed. The butterfly had needed this time of trial to develop and grow.

....

How should we deal with suffering?

- ✦ **Don't be surprised by it.**
  - *Beloved, think it not strange concerning the fiery trial which is to try you, as though some strange thing happened unto you.* (1 Peter 4:12)
  - *But of course you know that such troubles are a part of God's plan for us Christians.* (1 Thessalonians 3:3, TLB)

- ✦ **Keep a good attitude.**
  - *These things I have spoken unto you, that in me you might have peace. In the world you shall have tribulation: but be of good cheer; I have overcome the world.* (John 16:33)
  - *But rejoice, inasmuch as you are partakers of Christ's sufferings.* (1 Peter 4:13)
  - *And they departed from the presence of the council, rejoicing that they were **counted worthy** to suffer shame for his name.* (Acts 5:41) God doesn't let just anyone suffer. You have to be worthy.

- ✦ **Put it in perspective. Compare it to your reward in heaven.**
  - *For I reckon that the sufferings of this present time are not worthy to be compared with the glory which shall be revealed in us.* (Romans 8:18)
  - *For our light affliction, which is but for a moment, works for us a far more exceeding and eternal weight of glory.* (2 Corinthians 4:17)

- ✦ **Pray.**
  - *I have seen, I have seen the affliction of my people which is in Egypt, and I have heard their groaning, and am come down to deliver them.* (Acts 7:34)
  - *Many are the afflictions of the righteous: but the Lord delivers him out of them all.* (Psalm 34:19)
  - *The righteous cry, and **the Lord hears,** and delivers them out of all their troubles.* (Psalm 34:17)

Sample Lesson on Suffering

✦ **Remember that God will work it out.**
  - *"But the good man – what a different story! For the good man – the blameless, the upright, the man of peace – he has a wonderful future ahead of him.* **For him there is a happy ending.***"* (Psalm 37:37, The Living Bible)
  - *Weeping may endure for a night, but joy comes in the morning.* (Psalms 30:5)
  - *Humble yourselves therefore under the mighty hand of God, that he may exalt you in due time.* (1 Peter 5:5)

✦ **Remember that God uses everything, especially suffering, for our good.** *"And we know that all things work together for good to them that love God."* (Romans 8:28)

✦ **Transfer your concerns to Jesus.**
  "Casting all your care upon him; for he cares for you." (1 Peter 5:6)

✦ **Focus on the final outcome: the happiness that will be yours.**
  "Looking unto Jesus the author and finisher of our faith; who for the joy that was set before him endured the cross." (Hebrews 12:2)

✦ **Remember that the path to peace goes through suffering.** *"But the God of all grace, who has called us unto his eternal glory by Christ Jesus,* **after that you have suffered a while***, make you perfect, stablish, strengthen, settle you."* (1 Peter 5:10)

✦ **Embrace weakness.** Fasting may weaken us physically, but it builds us up spiritually.

Part 3: FEED

✦ **Put the suffering in perspective.**

- *For consider Him who endured such **hostility** from sinners against Himself, lest you become weary and discouraged in your souls. You have not yet resisted to bloodshed, striving against sin. (Hebrews 12:3-4, NKJV)*

- *By faith Moses, when he was come to years, refused to be called the son of Pharaoh's daughter; choosing rather to suffer affliction with the people of God, than to enjoy the pleasures of sin for a season; Esteeming the reproach of Christ greater riches than the treasures in Egypt: for he had respect unto the recompense of the reward. (Hebrews 11:24-26)*

✦ **Identify anything that is causing you to lose focus on God as you go through the pain.**

*So Peter went over the side of the boat and walked on the water toward Jesus. But when he **looked around** at the high waves, he was terrified and began to sink. (Matthew 14:29-30, TLB)*

✦ **Pray for help.**

- *"Save me, Lord! he shouted." **Instantly** Jesus reached out his hand and rescued him. (Matthew 14:31, TLB)*
- *Humble yourselves therefore under the mighty hand of God, that he may exalt you in due time: Casting all your care upon him; for he cares for you. (1 Peter 5:6-7)*

✦ **Recognize that it is an honor to suffer for your faith.**

And they departed from the presence of the council, rejoicing that they were counted worthy to suffer shame for his name. (Acts 5:41)

✦ **Pray for your friends.**

Then, when Job prayed for his friends, the Lord restored his wealth and happiness! In fact, the Lord gave him twice as much as before! (Job 42:10, TLB) By the way, have you thanked the Lord for the friends who prayed for you during your problems?

✦ **Praise God for his help.** *And when they began to sing and to praise, the Lord set ambushes against the children of Ammon. (2 Chronicles 20:22)*

Sample Lesson on Suffering

Part 4: DEED

✦ **Has the Lord just brought you through a time of trial and suffering?**

- **List three things you have learned from it.**

- **Have you thanked God for deliverance?** The book of Judges tells of a time when the Israelites were afflicted by Jabin, a Canaanite king, so they cried out to God and he delivered them. It is interesting that Judges devotes only one verse in Chapter 4 to their prayer, but 31 verses in Chapter 5 to their thanksgiving!

- **Have you gained confidence from your experience?**
  You have overcome the wicked one. (1 John 2:13)

- **Have you celebrated your victory?** *You will become slaves to your enemies because of your failure to praise God for all that he has given you.* (Deuteronomy 28:48, TLB)

✦ **Has your suffering encouraged other Christians?**
And because of my imprisonment many of the Christians here seem to have lost their fear of chains! ... and they have become more and more bold in telling others about Christ. (Philippians 1:12-14)

✦ **What two things could you have done better in your time of testing?**

✦ **Make a list of Christians who are being persecuted and pray for them.**
These may include people you do not know personally.

Chapter 27

Sample Lesson: Joy

Since Christ suffered and underwent pain, you must have the same attitude he did; you must be ready to suffer, too. (1 Peter 4:1)

Part 1: SEED

The biblical definition of the topic: joy.

The joy of the Lord is the abiding delight that emanates from the Holy Spirit living in and through you. Every Christian should experience the joy of the Lord because it is a fruit of the Spirit. *The fruit of the Spirit is love, joy, peace, long suffering, gentleness, goodness, faith, meekness, temperance.* (Galatians 5:22-23) The joy of the Lord is a gift of God to his children. *"You became followers of us, and of the Lord, having received the word in much affliction, with joy of the Holy Ghost."* (1 Thessalonians 1:6)

"For the kingdom of God is not meat and drink; but righteousness, and peace, and joy in the Holy Ghost." (Romans 14:17). You cannot experience the joy of the Lord and grieve the Spirit at the same time. As a result of his sin, King David lost the joy of his salvation. David knew only God could restore his joy. *"Restore unto me the joy of thy salvation."* (Psalm 51:12) Likewise the prodigal son's joy was quickly restored when he returned to his father. *"But the father said to his servants, 'Quick! Bring the best robe and put it on him. Put a ring on his finger and sandals on his feet. Bring the fattened calf and kill it. Let's have a feast and celebrate."* (Luke 15:22-23). Joy comes from obedience and being in the presence of God.

✦ **Joy is an experience shared among God, Jesus, the Holy Spirit, the angels, and Christians:**

The LORD shall rejoice in his works. (Psalm 104:31)

At that time Jesus, full of joy through the Holy Spirit, said, *"I praise you, Father, Lord of heaven and earth ..."* (Luke 10:21, NIV)

You received the word in much affliction, with the joy of the Holy Spirit. (1 Thessalonians 1:6)

Joy shall be in heaven over one sinner that repents. (Luke 15:7)

Whom having not seen, you love; in whom, though now you see him not, yet believing, you rejoice with joy unspeakable and full of glory. (1 Peter 1:8)

Part 2: NEED
The benefits of learning about joy.

✦ ***The joy of the Lord is your strength.* (Nehemiah 8:10)**

When a man is gloomy, everything seems to go wrong; when he is cheerful, everything seems right! (Proverbs 15:15, TLB)

✦ **We are commanded to rejoice in our salvation.**
Rejoice, because your names are written in heaven. (Luke 10:19-21)

Rejoice always. (2 Thessalonians 5:16-18)

In the day of prosperity be joyful. (Ecclesiastes 7:14)

✦ **Joy is the motivation by which Jesus endured suffering and received his eternal reward.**
"Looking unto Jesus the author and finisher of our faith; who for the joy that was set before him endured the cross, despising the shame, and is set down at the right hand of the throne of God." (Hebrews 12:2-3)

....

Pastor Craig Reynolds shared an illustration about the power of expectations. There were two workers who were told they had to work an eight hour day. But the supervisor told one of them that he would receive $100 while he told the other that he would receive a million dollars! Because of the great reward ahead, the one expecting a million dollars naturally maintained a good attitude and never complained. We Christians should remember that we have a joyful reward waiting for us in heaven.

....

✦ **The apostles rejoiced in their suffering.**
They departed from the presence of the council, rejoicing that they were counted worthy to suffer shame for his name. (Acts 5:41)

✦ **God is not pleased with those who fail to celebrate his blessings.**
Moreover all these curses shall come upon you ... because you serve not the LORD your God with joyfulness. (Deuteronomy 28:45)

Part 3: FEED
The characteristics of joy.

✦ Problems cannot crush joy.
Count it all joy, my brethren, when you encounter various trials. (James 1:2)
Why count it pure joy? James 1:3 tells us that our faith grows in difficult times. We are experiencing *"the fellowship of his sufferings."* (Philippians 3:10) We experience kinship with Jesus in suffering and find his strength in our weakness.

We rejoice in our sufferings, knowing that suffering produces endurance, and endurance produces character, and character produces hope, and hope does not put us to shame. (Romans 5:3-5, ESV)

✦ Circumstances cannot crush joy.
Happiness may depend on circumstances, but joy does not.
Now the God of hope fill you with all joy and peace in believing, that you may abound in hope, through the power of the Holy Ghost. (Romans 15:13)

✦ Joy is a characteristic of believers.

Be glad in the LORD, and rejoice, you righteous:
And shout for joy, all you that are upright in heart. (Psalm 32:11)

But let the righteous be glad; let them rejoice before God:
Yes, let them exceedingly rejoice. (Psalm 68:3)

✦ Believers express joy in exuberant ways.
But let all those that put their trust in you rejoice:
*Let them ever **shout for joy**, because you defend them:*
Let them also that love your name be joyful in you. (Psalm 5:11)

O clap your hands, all you people; Shout unto God with the voice of triumph. (Psalm 47:1)

✦ You find joy in the presence of God.
For you make him most blessed forever; you make him glad with the joy of your presence.
(Psalm 21:6, ESV)

You will show me the path of life: in your presence is fullness of joy. (Psalm 16:11)

✦ We don't have any reason to be depressed.

Why are you cast down, O my soul? and why are you disquieted in me? Hope in God: for I shall yet praise him. (Psalm 42:5).

Weeping may endure for a night, but joy comes in the morning. (Psalm 30:5)

Be of good cheer; I have overcome the world. (John 16:33)

Part 4: DEED
Do something with your knowledge.

1. Take notice of all the blessings you may have been overlooking.

2. Add a song to your next meeting.

3. Tell someone what the Lord has done for you.

4. Listen to someone else's testimony about the Lord's blessing.

5. Enjoy a good meal with loved ones. "Every man should eat and drink, and enjoy the good of all his labor, it is the gift of God." (Ecclesiastes 3:13)

6. Make someone's day with your smile and a kind word. "Heaviness in the heart of man makes it stoop: But a good word makes it glad. (Proverbs 12:25)

7. Don't get too busy or too tired to enjoy God's creation and to thank Him.

8. Don't sin, resulting in the temporary loss of joy.

9. Don't look for joy apart from God. Remain in his presence where there is fullness of joy.

10. Remember that you have an eternal home in heaven.

Chapter 28

Sample Lesson: GOD's Sovereignty

Part 1: SEED

The biblical definition of sovereignty.

✦ **God's sovereignty means that He is in supreme control over all creation: everyone and everything.**

The LORD has prepared his throne in the heavens; and his kingdom rules over all.
(Psalm 103:19)

He has done whatsoever he has pleased. (Psalm 115:3)

The LORD his God: which made heaven, and earth, the sea, and all that therein is.
(Psalm 146:5–6).

*For I know that the LORD **is** great, and **that** our Lord is above all gods. Whatsoever the LORD pleased, **that** did he in heaven, and in earth, In the seas, and all deep places. He causes the vapors to ascend from the ends of the earth;*
He makes lightnings for the rain; He brings the wind out of his treasuries. Who smote the firstborn of Egypt, both of man and beast. Who sent tokens and wonders into the midst of you, O Egypt, upon Pharaoh, and upon all his servants. Who smote great nations, And slew mighty kings.
(Psalm 135:5–10).

✦ **His dominion extends over every planet, every life, and every blade of grass.**

For of him, and through him, and to him, are all things. (Romans 11:36)

*For by him were all things created, that are in heaven, and that are in earth, visible and invisible, whether they be thrones, or dominions, or principalities, or powers: all things were created by him, and **for him**: And he is before all things, and by him all things consist. And he is the head of the body, the church: who is the beginning, the firstborn from the dead; that in **all** things he might have the preeminence. (Colossians 1:16-18)*

✦ **God's sovereign rule is forever.**

*How great **are** his signs! And how mighty **are** his wonders! His kingdom is an everlasting kingdom, and his dominion is from generation to generation. (Daniel 4:3)*

*Of the increase of **his** government and peace **there shall be** no end. (Isaiah 9:7)*

Part 2: NEED

Why do Christians need to understand God's sovereign control over the heavens and the earth?

✦ **If we understand that God rules over all things at all times, we can trust his will to come to pass, even if things do not appear to be going well.**

*Mark the perfect **man**, and behold the upright: For the end of **that** man **is** peace. (Psalm 37:37)*

Though he slay me, yet will I trust in him. (Job 13:15)

✦ **Even man's evil intents do not stop the purpose of God. In fact, God uses ill motives to promote the saints.**

You thought evil against me; but God meant it unto good. (Genesis 50:20)

But the more they afflicted them, the more they multiplied and grew. (Exodus 1:12)

And we know that all things work together for good to them that love God. (Romans 8:28)

✦ **God's sovereign rule protects Christians from getting into trouble.**

You are my hiding place from every storm of life; you even keep me from getting into trouble! (Psalm 32:7, TLB)

✦ **Knowing that God rules everything, we are encouraged that no area of our lives is apart from his control.**

*And there came a man of God, and spoke unto the king of Israel, and said, Thus says the LORD, Because the Syrians have said, The LORD **is** God of the hills, but he **is** not God of the valleys, therefore will I deliver all this great multitude into your hand, and you shall know that **I am** the LORD. (1 Kings 20:28)*

Part 3: FEED

What the Bible says about God's sovereign rule.

✦ **God controls eternity.**

Fear him which is able to destroy both soul and body in hell. (Matthew 10:28)

And Jesus said unto him, Verily I say unto you, today shall you be with me in paradise. (Luke 23:43)

✦ **God knows the future and controls the future.**

*I **am** God, and there is none like me, declaring the end from the beginning,* (Isaiah 46:9-10)

O Lord, I know it is not within the power of man to map his life and plan his course- so you correct me, Lord. (Jeremiah 10:23)

I will instruct you and teach you in the way which you shall go: I will guide you with my eye. (Psalms 32:8)

A man's heart devises his way: **but the Lord directs his steps**. (Proverbs 16:9)

The steps of a good man are ordered by the Lord: and he delights in his way. (Psalm 37:23)

*For he is our God; and we are the people of **his** pasture, and the sheep of **his** hand.* (Psalm 95:7)

He will show you things to come. (John 16:13)

What? know you not that your body is the temple of the Holy Ghost which is in you, which you have of God, and you are not your own? (1 Corinthians 6:19)

✦ **God, in his sovereignty, protects you.**

GOD guards you from every evil, he guards your very life. He guards you when you leave and when you return, he guards you now, he guards you always. (Psalm 121:7–8).

Be gracious to me, O God, be gracious to me, For my soul takes refuge in You; And in the shadow of Your wings I will take refuge until destruction passes by. (Psalm 57:1)

✦ God is in charge of leaders.

Lord, will you slay also a righteous nation? (Genesis 20:4).

*But the LORD was with Joseph, and showed him mercy, and **gave him favor** in the sight of the keeper of the prison.* (Genesis 39:21)

Please grant me success today by making the king favorable to me. Put it into his heart to be kind to me. (Nehemiah 1:11) *So it pleased the king to send me; and I set him a time.* (Nehemiah 2:6)

Because of his great power he rules forever. He watches every movement of the nations. (Psalm 66:7, TLB)

The king's heart is in the hand of the LORD, as the rivers of water: He turns it whithersoever he will. (Proverbs 21:1)

For this has been decreed by the messengers; it is commanded by the holy ones, so that everyone may know that the Most High rules over the kingdoms of the world. He gives them to anyone he chooses — even to the lowliest of people." (Daniel 4:17, NLT)

*For the kingdom **is** the LORD's: and he **is** the governor among the nations.* (Psalm 22:28)

✦ God rules over the weather.

As long as the earth remains, there will be planting and harvest, cold and heat, summer and winter, day and night." (Genesis 8:22, NLT)

He said to them, "Why are you afraid, you men of little faith?" Then He got up and rebuked the winds and the sea, and it became perfectly calm. The men were amazed, and said, "What kind of a man is this, that even the winds and the sea obey Him?" (Matthew 8:26-27)

He causes the clouds to arise from the end of the earth, makes lightning bolts accompany the rain, and brings the wind out of his storehouses. (Psalm 135:7, NET)

And the LORD turned a mighty strong west wind. (Exodus 10:19)

I sent rain on one town but withheld it from another. Rain fell on one field, while another field withered away. (Amos 4:7, NLT).

✦ God uses every circumstance.

But as for you, you thought evil against me; but God meant it unto good. (Genesis 50:20)

And we know that all things work together for good to them that love God. (Romans 8:28)

Sample Lesson on God's Sovereignty

*I am the vine, you are the branches: He that abides in me, and I in him, the same brings forth much fruit: for **without me you can do nothing.*** (John 15:5)

✦ **God's sovereignty does not remove your freedom to choose.**

Choose you this day whom you will serve. (Joshua 24:15)

The Lord is not slack concerning his promise, as some men count slackness; but is long suffering to us-ward, not willing that any should perish, but that all should come to repentance. (2 Peter 3:9)

Multitudes, multitudes in the valley of decision: for the day of the LORD is near in the valley of decision. (Joel 3:14).

I have set before you life and death, blessing and curse. Therefore choose life, that you and your offspring may live. (Deuteronomy 30:19, ESV)

How often would I have gathered your children together, even as a hen gathers her chickens under her wings, and you would not! (Matthew 23:37)

- God chose the angels, but one-third of them chose to rebel.
- God chose the Israelites, but many chose to worship idols.
- The Lord picked Judas, but he betrayed Jesus.
- One thief on the cross chose faith, the other refused.

Part 4: DEED
Application.

- Recall a time when things appeared to be going badly, but the situation ended wonderfully.
- Identify a current problem that does not look good. Remember that God is in charge of the outcome. Cheer up. Begin to thank him for all that he will accomplish.
- Keep three verses about God's sovereign rule. Carry them with you and read them three times a day. Expect your faith and peace to become stronger.
- Look at a past event. Can you see the good that came from it? For example, I knew a lady who had a car wreck. When the doctors scanned her brain, they identified and removed a cancerous tumor. What seemed to be a bad accident was actually a blessing in disguise.

Chapter 29

Sample Lesson: Divine Healing

Part 1: SEED

The Biblical Definition of Healing.

A. Healing is the restoration of health and/or wholeness to an afflicted individual. Such healing can apply to the mind and body.

It is possible for divine healing to occur in the body, while a separate healing may be required for the emotions. I knew of a Christian who was healed of cancer through prayer, but who continued to suffer from depression as a result of the anguish she had experienced.

B. God may heal supernaturally or through medical science, but all healing is divine healing.

Every good gift and every perfect gift is from above, and comes down from the Father of lights. (James 1:17) Medicine, vitamins, or surgery are each a "good gift" "from above."

C. Natural Healing

"And went to him, and bound up his wounds, pouring in oil and wine." (Luke 10:34).

Medicine does good. (Proverbs 17:22)

Luke was "the beloved physician." (Colossians 4:14)

D. Miraculous Healing.

Jesus healed ten lepers miraculously: "And it came to pass, that, as they went, they were cleansed. (Luke 17:14)

Then he anointed the man's eyes with the mud...So he went and washed and came back seeing. (John 9:7, ESV)

Jesus said to him, "Rise, take up your bed and walk." And immediately the man was made well, took up his bed, and walked. (John 5:8-9, NKJV)

Part 2: NEED

Why Learn about Healing?

A. We are commanded to know and do God's will.

Understand what the Lord wants you to do. (Ephesians 5:15-17)

Brethren, I would not that you should be ignorant. (1 Corinthians 10:1)

May he equip you with all you need for doing his will. (Hebrews 13:20-21)

My people are destroyed for lack of knowledge. (Hosea 4:6)

B. God wants you prosperous, healthy, and happy.

Beloved, I wish above all things that you may prosper and be in health, even as your soul prospers. (3 John 2).

C. There is no sickness or injury in heaven. God wants you well and happy.
"Your kingdom come. Your will be done on earth as it is in heaven." (Matthew 6:10)

D. We can know how to avoid sickness.
"There shall no evil befall you, neither shall any plague come near your dwelling." (Psalm 91:10)

E. Biblical knowledge increases your faith.
"Faith comes by hearing, and hearing by the Word of God." (Romans 10:17)

Part 3: FEED

What the Bible Says about Healing

A. It is easy for God to heal sickness.

God raised Lazarus from the dead. Sickness is no challenge whatsoever.

B. God answers prayers for healing, yet we may have to take action.

I have heard your prayer, I have seen your tears: behold, I will heal you. And Isaiah said, Take a lump of figs. And they took and laid it on the boil, and he recovered.
(2 Kings 20:5 and 7)

Is any sick among you? Let him call for the elders of the church; and let them pray over him, anointing him with oil in the name of the Lord: And the prayer of faith shall save the sick, and the Lord shall raise him up. (James 5:14-15)

Notice that the elders are to **anoint the sick** "in the name (authority) of the Lord." This shows that the name or authority of the Lord is higher and greater than the authority of the sickness. Jesus' name has authority over common colds, congestion, infection, headaches, cancer, and all other illnesses and diseases.

O LORD my God, I cried unto you, and you have healed me. (Psalm 30:2)

C. Some sickness is the result of sin: some is not.

See, you are well again. Stop sinning or something worse may happen to you.
(John 5:14, NIV)

His disciples asked Him, "Rabbi, who sinned, this man or his parents, that he would be born blind?" Jesus answered, "It was neither that this man sinned, nor his parents; but it was so that the works of God might be displayed in him." (John 9:1-3, NASB)

D. Jesus has total authority over every disease. Diseases have to obey the Lord's command. The centurion compared sicknesses to slaves.

*When Jesus returned to Capernaum, a Roman officer came and pleaded with him, "Lord, my young servant lies in bed, paralyzed and in terrible pain." Jesus said, "I will come and heal him." But the officer said, "Lord, I am not worthy to have you come into my home. **<u>Just say the word</u>** from where you are, and my servant will be healed. I know this because I am under the authority of my superior officer, and I have authority over my soldiers. I only need **<u>to say</u>**, 'Go,' and they go, or 'Come,' and they come. And if I say to **my slaves**, 'Do this,' they do it."*
(Matthew 8:5-9, NLT)

Sample Lesson on Divine Healing

E. Christians have the God-given authority of Christ. Believers can verbally rebuke diseases "in the name of the Lord" and command them to depart and not return. Are you exercising your authority as a king and a priest unto God? Have you used the authority of Jesus' name to banish disease? All the authority of heaven backs you up.

I assure you: Whatever you bind on earth is already bound in heaven, (Matthew 18:18)

He went and stood at her bedside and ordered the fever to leave her. The fever left her. (Luke 4:39, GNT).

F. God has creative power in his words.

For he spoke, and it was done. (Psalm 33:9)

G. God also has destructive power in his commands:

Master, behold, the fig tree which you cursed is withered away. (Mark 11:21)

H. Speak the Word of God against sickness.

And take the helmet of salvation, and the sword of the Spirit, which is the word of God. (Ephesians 6:17) *"Prophesy upon these bones, and say unto them, O you dry bones, hear **the word of the LORD**."* (Ezekiel 37:4). **Proclaim Bible verses over the sick**. *"For the word of God is quick, and powerful, and sharper than any two-edged sword.* (Hebrews 4:12). Do not be discouraged if healing is not immediate. The word of God is like rain that falls on a garden. Over time, the seeds sprout and the plants grow. *"For as the rain comes down, and the snow from heaven, and returns not thither, but waters the earth, and makes it bring forth and bud, that it may give seed to the sower, and bread to the eater: So shall my word be that goes forth out of my mouth: it shall not return unto me void, but **it shall accomplish that which I please**, and it shall prosper in the thing whereto I sent it.* (Isaiah 55:10-11). The Word of God will prevail. Just allow time.

I shall not die, but live, and declare the works of the LORD. (Psalm 118:17)

Let the redeemed of the LORD say so. (Psalm 107:2)

The LORD will sustain him on his sickbed; You will heal him on the bed where he lies. (Psalm 41:3)

Let the weak say, I am strong. (Joel 31:10)

I. God may provide healing through communion. There are many testimonies of the importance of the elements of communion in healing.

Who his own self bare our sins in his own body on the tree, that we, being dead to sins, should live unto righteousness: by whose stripes you were healed. (1 Peter 2:24). Because the wages of sin is death, Jesus' death paid for our sins. His sufferings, the lashes, as evidenced by the stripes on his back, paid the price for our sicknesses.

And as they were eating, Jesus took bread, and blessed it, and brake it, and gave it to the disciples, and said, Take, eat; this is my body. And he took the cup, and gave thanks, and gave it to them, saying, Drink all of it; For this is my blood of the new testament, which is shed for many for the remission of sins. (Matthew 26:26-28)

J. Jesus asks us an important question: "Do you want to be well?" Jesus wants the best for us. Do you?

"When Jesus saw him lying there and knew that he had already been there a long time, he said to him, "Do you want to be healed?" (John 5:6). *The desire to be healed is important. Do we want the healing to glorify God? Do we want to be whole and well; serving Jesus with all of our with all heart, soul, and mind?* (Matthew 22:37). *Do we want to have a testimony of the Lord's power?*

K. All those healed in the Bible had something in common: they all sought healing, or others sought healing on their behalf.

He began to shout, Jesus, Son of David, have mercy on me! (Mark 10:47)

Now when the sun was setting, all those who had any who were sick with various diseases brought them to him, and he laid his hands on every one of them and healed them. (Luke 4:40)

When he heard that Jesus had come from Judea to Galilee, he went and begged Jesus to come to Capernaum to heal his son, who was about to die. (John 4:47, NLT)

L. Ask Someone who can help you.

You have not, because you ask not. (James 4:2)

M. Our faith is important to receive healing.

They begged him to let the sick touch at least the fringe of his robe, and all who touched him were healed. (Matthew 14:36)

Jesus asked them, "Do you believe I can make you see?" "Yes, Lord," they told him, "we do." (Matthew 9:28)

Daughter, your faith has made you well. Go in peace. Your suffering is over. (Mark 5:34)

But when Jesus heard it, he answered him, saying, Fear not: believe only, and she shall be made whole. (Luke 8:50)

And he said to him, "Rise and go your way; your faith has made you well." (Luke 17:19)

O. Take steps to avoid sickness.

He said, "If you will listen carefully to the voice of the LORD your God and do what is right in his sight, obeying his commands and keeping all his decrees, then I will not make you suffer any of the diseases I sent on the Egyptians; for I am the LORD who heals you." (Exodus 15:26, NLT)

You must serve only the LORD your God. If you do, I will bless you with food and water, and I will protect you from illness. There will be no miscarriages or infertility in your land, and I will give you long, full lives. (Exodus 23;25, NLT)

Part 4: DEED

Application

1. Remember that God is honored when you are healed. God is pleased when you are prosperous.
    a. "Great is the LORD, who delights in the welfare of his servant!" (Pslam 35:27)
    b. Jesus said, *"This sickness will not end in death. No, it is **for God's glory** so that God's Son may be glorified through it."* (John 11:14, NIV)

2. Pray for healing for yourself or someone else. Your prayers move the hand of God.
    a. The effectual fervent prayer of a righteous man avails much. (James 5:16)
    b. Again I say to you that if two of you agree on earth concerning anything that they ask, it will be done for them by My Father in heaven. (Matthew 18:19)
    c. Until now you have not asked for anything in my name. Ask and you will receive, and your joy will be complete. (John 16:24)
    d. You can ask for anything in my name, and I will do it, so that the Son can bring glory to the Father. (John 14:13). Pray until something happens (PUSH). If you need to continue to pray and praise the Lord, wait on him with great assurance of an answer. We only wait on those we know will show up. "My soul, wait thou only upon God; for my expectation is from him. He only is my rock and my salvation: he is my defense; I shall not be moved." (Psalm 62:5-6). Pray thru!

3. Pray for your friends who are sick. "As for me, far be it from me that I should sin against the LORD by failing to pray for you." (1 Samuel 12:23)

4. Pray that you will not get sick. He brought them forth also with silver and gold: And there was not one feeble person among their tribes. (Psalm 105:37)

5. If you are sick, don't be too embarrassed to call for the elders of the church to anoint you and pray over you. "Is any sick among you? Let him call for the elders of the church; and let them pray over him, anointing him with oil in the name of the Lord: And the prayer of faith shall save the sick, and the Lord shall raise him up; and if he has committed sins, they shall be forgiven him. (James 5:14-15)

6. If there is sickness, verbally, curse the illness in the name, or authority of the Lord. Remember, Jesus silenced the fever and it departed. "And he stood over her, and rebuked the fever; and it left her." (Luke 4:39)

7. Thank God for his healing power and mercy. "Let all that I am praise the LORD; may I never forget the good things he does for me. He forgives all my sins and heals all my diseases. He redeems me from death." (Psalm 103:2-4, NLT)

8. Pronounce Bible verses over the sick. "Prophesy upon these bones, and say unto them, O you dry bones, hear the word of the LORD." (Ezekiel 37:4).
    a. I shall not die, but live, and declare the works of the LORD. (Psalm 118:17)
    b. Let the redeemed of the LORD say so. (Psalm 107:2)
    c. The LORD will sustain him on his sickbed; You will heal him on the bed where he lies. (Psalm 41:3)
    d. Let the weak say, I am strong. (Joel 31:10)

9. Thank God that Jesus has paid the price for your healing: he has taken your sicknesses from you and put them on himself.
    a. Surely he has borne our griefs and carried our sorrows. But he [was] wounded for our transgressions, [he was] bruised for our iniquities: the chastisement of our peace [was] upon him; and with his stripes we are healed. (Isaiah 53:4-5)
    b. He Himself bore our sins in His body on the cross, so that we might die to sin and live to righteousness; for by His wounds you were healed. (1 Peter 2:24)
    c. He took our illnesses and bore our diseases. (Matthew 8:17, ESV)
    d. Therefore God also has highly exalted him, and given him a name which is above every name. (Philippians 2:9)
    e. Far above all principality, and power, and might, and dominion, and every name that is named. (Ephesians 1:21)
    f. God has put all things under the authority of Christ. (Ephesians 1:22, TLB)

Chapter 30

Sample Lesson: Heaven

Part 1: SEED

The biblical definition of Heaven.

Heaven is the place of the thrown of God from which He rules over all things. It is where Christians will live together with God forever.

The LORD looks down from heaven. (Psalm 33:13)

✦ **God created Heaven.**

Abraham was confidently looking forward to a city with eternal foundations, a city designed and built by God. (Hebrews 11:10)

God is not ashamed to be called their God, for he has prepared a city for them. (Hebrews 11:16)

✦ **Heaven is "far better" than earth and something to yearn for and anticipate with excitement.**

For we know that the whole creation groans and travails in pain together until now. And not only they, but ourselves also, which have the first fruits of the Spirit, even we ourselves groan within ourselves, waiting for the adoption, to wit, the redemption of our body. (Romans 8:22-23)

For I am in a strait betwixt two, having a desire to depart, and to be with Christ; which is far better: (Philippians 1:23)

We are confident, I say, and willing rather to be absent from the body, and to be present with the Lord. (2 Corinthians 5:8)

For to me to live is Christ, and to die is gain. (Philippians 1:21)

Part 2: NEED

What does heaven have to do with me?

✦ **Knowing more about your eternal destination gives you strength and encouragement for the journey. Keep your eyes on the prize.**

Wherefore seeing we also are compassed about with so great a cloud of witnesses, let us lay aside every weight, and the sin which does so easily beset us, and let us run with patience the race that is set before us, Looking unto Jesus the author and finisher of our faith; who for the joy that was set before him endured the cross, despising the shame, and is set down at the right hand of the throne of God. For consider him that endured such contradiction of sinners against himself, lest you be wearied and faint in your minds. (Hebrews 12:1-3)

✦ **We can know more about Jesus by learning about of heaven.**

For example, we know that we receive a new, secret name in heaven. This tells us that Jesus wants a close personal relationship with each of us individually, not just as a member of a larger group.

Part 3: FEED

What the Bible says about Heaven.

✦ **Heaven is the place of God and his glory, Jesus, angels, and believers**.

But you are come unto mount Sion, and unto the city of the living God, the heavenly Jerusalem, and to an innumerable company of angels, To the general assembly and church of the firstborn, which are written in heaven, and to God the Judge of all, and to the spirits of just men made perfect, And to Jesus the mediator of the new covenant, and to the blood of sprinkling, that speaks better things than that of Abel. (Hebrews 12:22-24)

✦ **The human mind has not imagined how delightful heaven is.**

Eye has not seen, nor ear heard, neither have entered into the heart of man, the things which God has prepared for them that love him. (1 Corinthians 2:9)

Sample Lesson on Heaven

✦ Heaven has levels.

I know a man in Christ who fourteen years ago was caught up to the third heaven.
(2 Corinthians 12:2, NLT)

✦ Men cannot say some of the things which are said in heaven.

And I know that this man was caught up into paradise—whether in the body or out of the body I do not know, God knows— and he heard things that cannot be told, which man may not utter.
(2 Corinthians 12:3-4, NLT)

✦ Heaven is a place of loud worship.

I saw the Lord. He was sitting on a lofty throne, and the train of his robe filled the Temple. Attending him were mighty seraphim, each having six wings. With two wings they covered their faces, with two they covered their feet, and with two they flew. They were calling out to each other,
"Holy, holy, holy is the LORD of Heaven's Armies!
The whole earth is filled with his glory!"
Their voices shook the Temple to its foundations, and the entire building was filled with smoke.
(Isaiah 6:1-4, NLT)

✦ The Lord will give you a new, glorified body.

We, too, wait with eager hope for the day when God will give us our full rights as his adopted children, including the new bodies he has promised us. (Romans 8:23, NLT)

We look for the Saviour, the Lord Jesus Christ: who shall change our vile body, that it may be fashioned like unto his glorious body. (Philippians 3:20-21)

And as we have borne the image of the earthy, **we shall also bear the image of the heavenly.**
Now this I say, brethren, that flesh and blood cannot inherit the kingdom of God; neither does corruption inherit incorruption. Behold, I show you a mystery; We shall not all sleep, but we shall all be changed,
In a moment, in the twinkling of an eye, **at the last trump**: *for the trumpet shall sound, and the dead shall be raised incorruptible, and we shall be changed.*
For this corruptible must put on incorruption, and this mortal must put on immortality.
(1 Corinthians 15:41-53)

✦ We will know God like He knows us.

For now we see through a glass, darkly; but then face to face: now I know in part; but then shall I know even as also I am known. (1 Corinthians 13:12)

✦ You will be with Jesus forever.

When everything is ready, I will come and get you, so that you will always be with me where I am. (John 14:3, NLT)

✦ Those who martyred for the Lord will receive a special robe.

You have a few names even in Sardis which have not defiled their garments; and **they shall walk with me in white: for they are worthy.** *(Revelation 3:4)*

And white robes were given unto every one of them; and it was said unto them, that they should rest yet for a little season, until their fellow servants also and their brethren, that should be killed as they were, should be fulfilled. (Revelation 6:11)

After this I beheld, and, lo, a great multitude, which no man could number, of all nations, and kindreds, and people, and tongues, stood before the throne, and before the Lamb, clothed with white robes, and palms in their hands. (Revelation 7:9-10)

And one of the elders answered, saying unto me, What are these which are arrayed in white robes? and whence came they?
And I said unto him, Sir, you know. And he said to me, These are they which came out of great tribulation, and have washed their robes, and made them white in the blood of the Lamb. Therefore are they before the throne of God, and **serve him day and night in his temple**: *and* **he that sits on the throne shall dwell among them.** (Revelation 7:13-17)

✦ The Lord will give each of us a crown!

I have fought a good fight, I have finished my course, I have kept the faith:
Henceforth there is laid up for me a **crown of righteousness**, *which the Lord, the righteous judge, shall give me at that day: and not to me only, but unto* **all** *them also that love his appearing.*
(2 Timothy 4:7-8)

… be thou faithful unto death, and I will give thee a **crown of life**. (Revelation 2:10)

✦ The Lord will reward you with unspeakable rewards!

And the nations were angry, and your wrath is come, and the time of the dead, that they should be judged, and that **you should give reward unto your servants the prophets, and to the saints, and them that fear your name, small and great;** *and should destroy them which destroy the earth.* (Revelation 11:18)

And, behold, I come quickly; and **my reward is with me**, *to give every man according as his work ….* (Revelation 22:12)

But as it is written, Eye has not seen, nor ear heard, neither have entered into the heart of man, the things which God has prepared for them that love him. (1 Corinthians 2:9)

*I knew a man in Christ above fourteen years ago, (whether in the body, I cannot tell; or whether out of the body, I cannot tell: God knows;) such an one caught up to **the third heaven.***
And I knew such a man, (whether in the body, or out of the body, I cannot tell: God knows;)
How that he was caught up into paradise, and heard unspeakable words, which it is not lawful for a man to utter. *(2 Corinthians 12:2-4)*

✦ **In heaven, people do not marry nor continue to be married.**

For in the resurrection they neither marry, nor are given in marriage, but are as the angels of God in heaven. (Matthew 22:30)

✦ **You will reign with Christ.**

If we endure hardship, we will reign with him. (2 Timothy 2:12, NLT)

*Master, I invested your money and made ten times the original amount!' " 'Well done!' the king exclaimed. 'You are a good servant. You have been faithful with the little I entrusted to you, **so you will be governor of ten cities as your reward.**' "The next servant reported, 'Master, I invested your money and made five times the original amount.' " 'Well done!' the king said. 'You will be governor over five cities.'* (Luke 19:16-19, NLT)

✦ **The Lord will appoint you as a judge.**

But that which you have already hold fast till I come.
*And he that overcomes, and keeps my works unto the end, to him will I give **power over the nations**: And he shall rule them with a rod of iron; as the vessels of a potter shall they be broken to shivers: even as I received of my Father.*
And I will give him the morning star. *(Revelation 25-28)*

Know you not that we shall judge angels? (1 Corinthians 6:3)

Then answered Peter and said unto him, Behold, we have forsaken all, and followed you; what shall we have therefore?
And Jesus said unto them, Verily I say unto you, That you which have followed me, in the regeneration when the Son of man shall sit in the throne of his glory, you also shall sit upon twelve thrones, judging the twelve tribes of Israel.
And every one that has forsaken houses, or brethren, or sisters, or father, or mother, or wife, or children, or lands, for my name's sake, shall receive an hundredfold, and shall inherit everlasting life. (Matthew 19:27-29)

✦ **You will be recognized and honored if you obeyed and taught God's commandments. Jesus will affirm that you belong to Him before God and the angels.**

Whosoever therefore shall break one of these least commandments, and shall teach men so, he shall be called the least in the kingdom of heaven: but whosoever shall do and teach them, the same shall be called great in the kingdom of heaven. (Matthew 5:19)

He that overcomes, the same shall be clothed in white raiment; and I will not blot out his name out of the book of life, but I will confess his name before my Father, and before his angels. (Revelation 3:5)

✦ **You will receive a new secret name.**

To him that overcomes will I give to eat of the hidden manna, and will give him a white stone, and in the stone a new name written, which no man knows saving he that receives it. (Revelation 2:17)

✦ **The Lord will go to the wedding supper of Jesus.**

And he says unto me, Write, Blessed are they which are called unto the marriage supper of the Lamb. (Revelation 19:9)

✦ **You will remain in the presence of God forever!**

Him that overcomes will I make a pillar in the temple of my God, and he shall go no more out: and I will write upon him the name of my God, and the name of the city of my God, which is new Jerusalem, which comes down out of heaven from my God: and I will write upon him my new name. (Revelation 3:12)

✦ **God will remember and reward each and every good deed, so keep serving Him.**

And remember that your heavenly Father to whom you pray has no favorites when he judges. He will judge you with perfect justice for everything you do; so act in reverent fear of him from now on until you get to heaven. (1 Peter 1:17)

*Behold, I come quickly: **hold that fast** which you have, that no man take your crown.* (Revelation 3:11)

✦ **You will not have any hunger, thirst, sadness, discomfort, pain or fatigue. You will live forever.**

*They shall hunger no more, neither thirst any more; neither shall the sun light on them, nor any heat. For the Lamb which is in the midst of the throne shall feed them, and shall lead them unto living fountains of waters: and **God shall wipe away all tears from their eyes.*** (Revelation 7:17)

And I heard a voice from heaven saying unto me, Write, Blessed are the dead which die in the Lord from henceforth: Yea, says the Spirit, that they may rest from their labors; and their works do follow them. (Revelation 14:13)

And God shall wipe away all tears from their eyes; and there shall be **no more death, neither sorrow, nor crying, neither shall there be any more pain**: *for the former things are passed away. And he that sat upon the throne said, Behold, I make all things new.* (Revelation 21:4-5)

✦ **You will live in a mansion designed and built for you.**

*In my Father's house are many mansions: if it were not so, I would have told you.
I go to prepare a place for you.* (John 14:2)

Part 4: DEED

Applying your knowledge of heaven.

✦ **From the verses in Revelation, what can you discern about the character of Jesus?**

✦ **List 10 things you know about eternity, such as the fact that "God shall wipe away all tears."**

And God shall wipe away all tears from their eyes; and there shall be no more death, neither sorrow, nor crying, neither shall there be any more pain: for the former things are passed away.
(Revelation 21:4) **Compare these experiences to life here. How does this affect the way you live?**

✦ **Do you have more family members in heaven or on earth?**

✦ **List five things that you expect to love the most about heaven.**

✦ **List five things you will be glad to leave behind.**

✦ **When you are in heaven, do you expect to think about earth much?**

✦ **Since Christians will be given responsibility to reign and rule with Christ, are you preparing for this responsibility? How?**

If we endure hardship, we will reign with him. (2 Timothy 2:12, NLT)

Master, I invested your money and made ten times the original amount!' " 'Well done!' the king exclaimed. 'You are a good servant. You have been faithful with the little I entrusted to you, **so you will be governor of ten cities as your reward.***'*
"The next servant reported, 'Master, I invested your money and made five times the original amount.' " 'Well done!' the king said. 'You will be governor over five cities.' (Luke 19:16-19, NLT)

The servant who made ten times the original amount was awarded ten cities.
The servant who made five times the original amount was awarded five cities.
Do you think that your heavenly responsibilities will be in proportion to your work on earth?

Chapter 31

Sample Lesson: Money Management

PART 1: SEED

Definition.

We are overseers of the resources God provides. God is the true owner. We honor God through adherence to his wisdom and guidance in financial affairs.

✦ **Christians are managers of God's money.**

The LORD God placed the man in the Garden of Eden to tend and watch over it. (Genesis 2:15)

For it will be like a man going on a journey, who called his servants and entrusted to them his property. (Matthew 25:14, ESV)

✦ **God owns everything we have.**

For every beast of the forest is mine, and the cattle upon a thousand hills. I know all the fowls of the mountains: and the wild beasts of the field are mine. If I were hungry, I would not tell you: For the world is mine, and the fullness thereof. (Psalm 50:10-12)

✦ **God provides plenty of guidance about money management.**

I am the LORD your God, who teaches you to profit, who leads you in the way you should go. (Isaiah 48:17)

✦ The secret to money management.

The secret to money management is staying on the Vine: living in Christ. When we seek Him first, "all these things shall be added unto you." (Matthew 6:33)

I am the vine, you are the branches: He that abides in me, and I in him, the same brings forth much fruit: for without me you can do nothing. (John 15:5)

A man can receive nothing, except it be given him from heaven. (John 3:27)
Godliness is profitable unto all things, having promise of the life that now is, and of the life to come. (1 Timothy 4:8)

✦ Appoint God as your Chief Financial Officer: the Sovereign over your wealth.

The battle is not yours, but God's. (2 Chronicles 20:15)

Casting all your care upon him; for he cares for you. (1 Peter 5:7)

The blessing of the Lord, it makes rich, and he adds no sorrow to it. (Proverbs 10:22)

My heart cries our within me; **how I long to help you***! (Hosea 11:8)*

Always be expecting much from him, your God. (Hosea 12:6, TLB)

✦ If you lead a righteous life, God will provide for you.

I have been young and now am old; yet have I not seen the righteous forsaken nor his seed begging bread. (Psalm 37:25)

The LORD is my shepherd; I have all that I need. (Psalm 23:1)

Both riches and honor come from you, and you rule over all. (I Chronicles 29:12)

Mark the perfect man, and behold the upright: for the end of that man is peace. (Psalm 37:37)

Part 2: NEED

Why Learn About Money Management?

✦ **To know that God is pleased when you prosper.**

Let the LORD be magnified, which has pleasure in the prosperity of his servant. (Psalm 35:27)

The very hairs of your head are all numbered. So don't worry! (Matthew 10:30-31, TLB)

When you produce much fruit, you are my true disciples. This brings great glory to my Father. (John 15:8, NLT)

✦ **To know that, sometimes, we display our faith by waiting for God. We only wait for those we know will come through. While we wait for God to act, praise him for his care for us and thank him for the coming blessings.**

*But they that **wait** upon the LORD shall renew their strength; they shall mount up with wings as eagles; they shall run, and not be weary; and they shall walk, and not faint. (Isaiah 40:31)*

✦ **To remember that doing things God's way is not hard.**

His commandments are not burdensome. (1 John 5:3, NLT)

✦ **To know that failure comes dishonoring God.**

*If you don't do **your best** for him, he will pay you in a way that you won't like. (Ephesians 3:25, TLB)*

An athlete is not crowned unless he competes according to the rules. (2 Timothy 2:5, ESV)

I ruined your crops by holding back the rain. (Amos 4:7)

For God shall bring every work into judgment, with every secret thing, whether it be good, or whether it be evil. (Ecclesiastes 12:14)

Except the LORD build the house, they labor in vain that build it. (Psalm 127:1)

No one, regardless of how shrewd or well-advised he is, can stand against the Lord. (Proverbs 21:30, TLB)

✦ **We need to know that wealth, in itself, cannot bring happiness.**

The foolishness of thinking that wealth brings happiness! (Ecclesiastes 5:10, TLB)

✦ **The benefits of learning sound money management are:**

God commands us to use His money wisely. This is an opportunity to serve and honor God.

✦ **We will be held accountable for how we use God's money.**

So then every one of us shall give account of himself to God. (Romans 14:12)

After a long time their master returned from his trip and called them to give an account of how they had used his money. (Matthew 25:19, NLT)

For unto whomsoever much is given, of him shall be much required: and to whom men have committed much, of him they will ask the more. (Luke 12:48)

✦ **If we use God's money wisely, God will commend us.**

The master was full of praise. 'Well done, my good and faithful servant.' (Matthew 25:21, NLT)

✦ **If we prove to be wise money managers, God will reward us with more money.**

✦ **God will give us greater rewards: including "true riches" (eternal riches).**

*You have been faithful in handling this small amount, so **now I will give you many more responsibilities**. Let's celebrate together!* (Matthew 25:21, NLT)

*If then you have not been faithful in the unrighteous wealth, who will entrust to you the **true riches**?* (Luke 16:11, ESV)

"One who is faithful in a very little is also faithful in much, and one who is dishonest in a very little is also dishonest in much. (Luke 16:10, ESV)

✦ **God will bless you so that you can be a blessing.**

For God is the one who provides seed for the farmer and then bread to eat. In the same way, he will provide and increase your resources and then produce a great harvest of generosity in you.
(2 Corinthians 9:10, NLT).

✦ **You will have more fun through giving.**

You're far happier giving than getting. (Acts 20:35, The Message)

Sample Lesson on Money Management

✦ We will avoid stress.

Take no thought for your life, what you shall eat, or what you shall drink; nor yet for your body, what you shall put on. Is not the life more than meat, and the body than raiment? Behold the fowls of the air: for they sow not, neither do they reap, nor gather into barns; yet your heavenly Father feeds them. Are you not much better than they? (Matthew 6:25-26)

✦ You will have financial freedom.

Money gives everything! (Ecclesiastes 10:19, NLT)

✦ You will avoid financial bondage.

The rich rules over the poor, and the borrower is servant to the lender. (Proverbs 22:7).

✦ We will avoid financial ruin.

*Then you ought to have invested my money with the bankers, and at my coming I should have received what was my own with interest. So take the talent from him and give it to him who has the ten talents. For to everyone who has will more be given, and he will have an abundance. But from the one who has not, **even what he has will be taken away**.*
(Matthew 25:27-29, ESV)

A little extra sleep, a little more slumber, a little folding of the hands to rest— then poverty will pounce on you like a bandit; scarcity will attack you like an armed robber.
(Proverbs 24:3-34, NLT)

But if any provide not for his own, and especially for those of his own house, he has denied the faith, and is worse than an infidel. (1 Timothy 5:8)

By much slothfulness the building decays; and through idleness of the hands the house drops through. (Ecclesiastes 10:18)

And the Lord said, "Who then is the faithful and wise manager, whom his master will set over his household, to give them their portion of food at the proper time? Blessed is that servant whom his master will find so doing when he comes. Truly, I say to you, he will set him over all his possessions. But if that servant says to himself, 'My master is delayed in coming,' and begins to beat the male and female servants, and to eat and drink and get drunk, the master of that servant will come on a day when he does not expect him and at an hour he does not know, and will cut him in pieces and put him with the unfaithful.
(Luke 12:42-46, ESV)

✦ You will be able to leave your grandchildren wealth.

A good man leaves an inheritance to his children's children. (Proverbs 13:22)

Part 3: FEED

What the Bible Says About Money Management.

✦ **Be thankful for what God has given you.**

Every good gift and every perfect gift is from above, coming down from the Father of lights with whom there is no variation or shadow due to change. (James 1:17, ESV)

✦ **Be content with what God has given you.**

I have learned, in whatsoever state I am, therewith to be content. (Philippians 4:11)

✦ **We should acknowledge God in financial matters. Ask him for help and direction. Make sure your money honors God!**

Seek his will in all you do, and he will show you which path to take. (Proverbs 3:6, NLT)

Commit your work to the LORD, and your plans will be established. (Proverbs 16:3, ESV)

Yet you don't have what you want because you don't ask God for it. And even when you ask, you don't get it because your motives are all wrong—you want only what will give you pleasure. (James 4:2-3, NLT)

✦ **Be ethical in your dealings. Make your payments on time.**

He who gains by oppressing the poor ... shall end in poverty. (Proverbs 22:16 Living Bible)

Don't cheat your neighbor by moving the ancient boundary markers set up by previous generations. (Proverbs 22:28, NLT)

God delights in those who keep their promises, and abhors those who don't. (Proverbs 12:22, TLB)

✦ **Giving first fruit offerings brings in more. Thereafter, on-going giving displays thanks, obedience, and trust.**

The first of the first fruits of your land you shall bring into the house of the LORD your God. (Exodus 23:19).

Honor the LORD with thy substance, and with the firstfruits of all your increase: So shall your barns be filled with plenty, and your presses shall burst out with new wine. (Proverbs 3:9-10)

*You must each decide in your heart how much to give. And don't give reluctantly or <u>**in response to pressure**</u>. "For God loves a person who gives cheerfully." And God will generously provide all you need. Then you will always have everything you need and plenty left over to share with others.* (2 Corinthians 9:7-8, NLT)

✦ **Maintain God as your first and highest priority. Neither money nor power should be a close second. The question is "Who, or what, am I living for?"**

*No one can serve two masters. For you will hate one and love the other; you will be devoted to one and despise the other. You **cannot** serve both God and money.* (Matthew 6:24)

But seek first the kingdom of God and his righteousness, and all these things will be added to you. (Matthew 6:33, ESV)

*But God said unto him, You fool, this night your soul shall be required of you: then whose shall those things be, which you have provided? <u>**So is he that lays up treasure for himself, and is not rich toward God.**</u>* (Luke 12:20–21).

✦ **Include Jesus in your financial plans, and you receive peace.**

And he went up unto them into the ship; and the wind ceased: and they were sore amazed in themselves beyond measure, and wondered. (Mark 6:51).

✦ **Avoid "Get Rich Quick" schemes.**

Whatever you do, work heartily, as for the Lord and not for men, (Colossians 3:23)

But people who long to be rich fall into temptation and are trapped by many foolish and harmful desires that plunge them into ruin and destruction. (1 Timothy 6:9, NLT)

Wealth from get-rich-quick schemes quickly disappears; wealth from hard work grows over time. (Proverbs 13:11, NLT)

Good planning and hard work lead to prosperity, but hasty shortcuts lead to poverty. (Proverbs 21:5, NLT)

A faithful man shall abound with blessings: But he that makes haste to be rich shall not be innocent. (Proverbs 28:20)

Part 4: DEED

Now that You Know, What Do You Do?

✦ **Ask God for financial wisdom.**

If any of you lack wisdom, let him ask of God, that gives to all men liberally, and upbraids not; and it shall be given him. (James 1:5-6)

✦ **When God gives you wisdom, act on it! Do what He impresses upon you to do. Putting a budget into a computer is different than putting it into your life. Plan your spending and buy only the things in your plan.**

But be you doers of the word, and not hearers only, deceiving your own selves. (James 1:22)

But don't begin until you count the cost. *For who would begin construction of a building without first calculating the cost to see if there is enough money to finish it? Otherwise, you might complete only the foundation before running out of money, and then everyone would laugh at you. (Luke 14:28-30)*

✦ **Ask God for a new level of prosperity.**

Now unto him that is able to do exceeding abundantly above all that we ask or think, according to the power that works in us. (Ephesians 3:20)

✦ **Enjoy doing a good job.**

Whatsoever your hand finds to do, do it with your might. (Ecclesiastes 9:10)

Work brings profit, but mere talk leads to poverty! (Proverbs 14:23)

Let not your hands be slack. (Zephaniah 3:16)

Do you see any truly competent workers? They will serve kings rather than working for ordinary people. (Proverbs 22:29, NLT)

✦ Keep it up.

Let us not be weary in well doing: for in due season we shall reap, if we faint not. (Galatians 6:9)

Lazy people are soon poor; hard workers get rich. (Proverbs 10:4)

Work hard and become a leader; be lazy and become a slave. (Proverbs 12:24, NLT)

✦ Ask God to make "all grace" abound to you.

And God is able to make all grace abound toward you, that you, always having all sufficiency in all things, may abound in every good work. (2 Corinthians 9:8)

✦ Ask God to send prosperity now.

*Save now, I beseech you, O LORD: O LORD, I beseech you, **send now prosperity**.* (Psalm 118:25)

If you abide in me, and my words abide in you, you shall ask what you will, and it shall be done unto you. (John 15:7)

✦ Ask God to send a financial angel.

Behold, I send an Angel before you, to keep you in the way, and to bring you into the place which I have prepared. (Exodus 23:20)

The LORD, before whom I walk, will send his angel with you, and prosper your way. (Genesis 24:40)

✦ Ask God to give you the strength to retain the wealth He provides.

Strong men retain riches. (Proverbs 11:16)

Don't agree to guarantee another person's debt or put up security for someone else. If you can't pay it, even your bed will be snatched from under you. (Proverbs 22:26-27, NLT)

Get security from someone who guarantees a stranger's debt. Get a deposit if he does it for foreigners. (Proverbs 20:16, NLT).

✦ Do not fall behind on any financial obligations.

Owe no man any thing, but to love one another. (Romans 13:8)

✦ Consider real estate. Cash and stocks are easy to liquidate and spend

Will you set your eyes upon that which is not? for riches certainly make themselves wings; they fly away as an eagle toward heaven. (Proverbs 23:5)

How long are you slack to go to possess the land, which the LORD God of your fathers has given you? (Joshua 18:3)

The land you have given me is a pleasant land. What a wonderful inheritance! (Psalm 16:6, NLT)

She considers a field, and buys it: With the fruit of her hands she plants a vineyard. (Proverbs 31:16)

Tell those who are rich not to be proud and not to trust in their money, which will soon be gone, but their pride and trust should be in the living God who always richly gives us all we need for our enjoyment. (1 Timothy 6:17)

✦ Save some money for unexpected opportunities. (But don't save too much).

The wise have wealth and luxury, but fools spend whatever they get. (Proverbs 21:20)
One gives freely, yet grows all the richer; another withholds what he should give, and only suffers want. (Proverbs 11:24, ESV)

✦ Do it God's way: ethically.

But if you refuse to listen to the LORD your God and do not obey all the commands and decrees I am giving you today, all these curses will come and overwhelm you:
    Your towns and your fields will be cursed.
    Your fruit baskets and breadboards will be cursed.
    Your children and your crops will be cursed.
    The offspring of your herds and flocks will be cursed.
    Wherever you go and whatever you do, you will be cursed.
"The LORD himself will send on you curses, confusion, and frustration in everything you do, until at last you are completely destroyed for doing evil and abandoning me.
(Deuteronomy 28:15-20, TLB)

You destroy all who are unfaithful to you. (Psalm 73:27)

✦ Keep your eyes on the prize.

"The master was full of praise. 'Well done, my good and faithful servant. You have been faithful in handling this small amount, so now I will give you many more responsibilities. Let's celebrate together! (Matthew 25:21, ESV0

Chapter 32

Sample Lesson: Taking the Name of God in Vain.

Part 1: SEED

Defining the subject

Taking the name of God: speaking God's name in an insignificant, frivolous, thoughtless, or careless manner; not according the reverence, honor and majesty of God Almighty. This may occur in terms that resemble God's name or in speaking God's name as a form of cursing. Doing so, or endorsing this, dishonors God.

Who has ascended to heaven and come down? Who has gathered the wind in his fists? Who has wrapped up the waters in a garment? Who has established all the ends of the earth? What is his name, and what is his son's name? Surely you know! (Proverbs 30:4)

✦ **God Himself defined His Name by these words to Moses:**

And the LORD descended in the cloud, and stood with him there, and proclaimed the name of the LORD. And the LORD passed by before him, and proclaimed,
The LORD, The LORD God,

1. *merciful and gracious,*

2. *long suffering,*

3. *and abundant in goodness and truth,*

4. *Keeping mercy for thousands,*

5. *forgiving iniquity and transgression and sin,*

6. *and that will by no means clear the guilty;*
   visiting the iniquity of the fathers upon the children, and upon the children's children, unto the third and to the fourth generation. (EXODUS 34:5-7)

Part 2: NEED

Why is this information critical?

✦ **There is great danger for this offense.**

You shall not take the name of the LORD your God in vain, for the LORD will not hold him guiltless who takes his name in vain. (Exodus 20:7, ESV)

✦ **A person who dishonors God's name is a person of poor character and ignorance.**
Billy Graham said that those who use God's name in vain do not respect the Lord.

Your enemies misuse your name. (Psalm 139:20)

Death and life are in the power of the tongue. (Proverbs 18:21).

✦ **Christians who use the name of the Lord in vain degrade themselves!**
When we dishonor Christ, the name by whom we are identified, we dishonor ourselves!

I am called by your name, O LORD, God of hosts. (Jeremiah 15:15)

Don't be misled—you cannot mock the justice of God. You will always harvest what you plant. (Galatians 6:7)

✦ **Words reveal what is in the heart.**

*But those things which proceed out of the mouth come forth **<u>from the heart</u>**; and they defile the man. For out of the heart proceed evil thoughts, murders, adulteries, fornications, thefts, false witness, **blasphemies**: These are the things which defile a man. (Matthew 15:18-20)*

Sample Lesson on Taking the Name of God in Vain

Part 3: FEED

What does the Bible say about this?

✦ **GOD has exalted his name and his Word above all!**

You have exalted above all things your name and your word. (Psalm 138:2)

"Our Father, who is in Heaven, hallowed is your name."
Hallowed: high, holy, exalted, sacred consecrated, sanctified, **consecrated as holy**, greatly revered and greatly honored.

✦ **True believers love the name of the LORD.**

*But let all who take refuge in you rejoice; let them ever sing for joy, and spread your protection over them, that **those who love your name** may exult in you.* (Psalm 5:11)

✦ **God's eternal name, I AM, is to be revered by all generations.**

*I AM has sent me unto you… The LORD God of your fathers, the God of Abraham, the God of Isaac, and the God of Jacob, has sent me unto you: **this is my name for ever, and this is my memorial unto all generations**.* (Exodus 3:14-15)

✦ **The name of the Lord has power and authority.**

Some trust in chariots and some in horses, but we trust in the name of the LORD our God.
They collapse and fall, but we rise and stand upright. (Psalm 20:7-8)

✦ **The name of the Lord is awe-inspiring.**

What a holy, awe-inspiring name he has! Fear of the LORD is the foundation of true wisdom.
All who obey his commandments will grow in wisdom. (Psalm 111:9-10)

✦ **The name of the LORD represents his character as Protector.**

The name of the LORD is a strong tower; the righteous man runs into it and is safe. (Proverbs 18:10)

◆ **God created all things, including our speech, for his glory and honor. Does your speech honor God?**

For from him and through him and for him are all things. (Romans 11:36, NIV)

For in him all things were created: things in heaven and on earth, visible and invisible, whether thrones or powers or rulers or authorities; all things have been created through him and for him. (Colossians 1:16)

Part 4: DEED
How should we use the name of the Lord?

◆ **ANYTIME you say the Lord's name, it is significant. Speak the name of the LORD wisely.**

When believers pray in Jesus' name, God accepts the request.
When the saints mention the name of Jesus, angels come to attention.
When Christians speak Jesus' name, devils tremble.
When God's children use the name of the Lord, storms subside, illnesses dry up.

◆ **Do not allow the pervasiveness of sinful language influence your speech.**

Do not bring shame on the name of your God by using it to swear falsely. (Leviticus 19:12)

Don't copy the behavior and customs of this world, but let God transform you into a new person by changing the way you think. Then you will learn to know God's will for you, which is good and pleasing and perfect. (Romans 12:2)

Then we will no longer be immature like children. (Ephesians 4:14)

All who belong to the LORD must turn away from evil. (2 Timothy 2:19)

◆ **Like Jesus, maintain reverence for God's name.**

Our Father in heaven, may your name be kept holy. (Matthew 6:9, NLT)

Sample Lesson on Taking the Name of God in Vain

✦ We should speak only words that honor God and build up one another.

Let no corrupt communication proceed out of your mouth, but that which is good to the use of edifying, that it may minister grace unto the hearers. And grieve not the Holy Spirit of God, whereby you are sealed unto the day of redemption. Let all bitterness, and wrath, and anger, and clamor, and evil speaking, be put away from you. (Ephesians 4:29-31)

✦ Lift up and praise the name of the Lord.

I will proclaim the name of the LORD; ascribe greatness to our God! (Deuteronomy 32:3)

So will I ever sing praises to your name. (Psalm 61:8)

✦ Praise the name of the LORD.

Sing to God, sing praises to his name; lift up a song to him who rides through the deserts; his name is the LORD; exult before him! (Psalm 68:4)

I will praise you, LORD, with all my heart; I will tell of all the marvelous things you have done. I will be filled with joy because of you. I will sing praises to your name, O Most High. (Psalm 9:1-2)

Chapter 33

Sample Lesson: Interpersonal Communications

Part 1: SEED

Definition.

We communicate all the time. We communicate verbally, in writing, through actions, facial expressions, body language, appearance, images, and tone of voice. We also communicate by what we do not say.

Part 2: NEED
Why study communications?

✦ **Because we live in community and in the information age, we spend most of our time communicating. Shouldn't we do it well?**

If you claim to be religious but don't control your tongue, you are fooling yourself, and your religion is worthless. (James 1:26)

And whatsoever you do, do it heartily, as to the Lord. (Colossians 3:23)

Beautiful words fill my mind, as I compose this song for the king.
Like the pen of a good writer my tongue is ready with a poem.
(Psalm 45:1, Good News Bible)

✦ **Words are powerful. Sound speech can promote you.**

Death and life are in the power of the tongue. (Proverbs 18:21)

All were speaking well of him, and were amazed at the gracious words coming out of his mouth. (Luke 4:22)

Sample Lesson on Interpersonal Communications

✦ There's blessing in following God's instructions.

But if you look carefully into the perfect law that sets you free, and if you do what it says and don't forget what you heard, then God will bless you for doing it. (James 1:25)

✦ You can do great things for God's Kingdom and help others through your speech.

A person finds joy in giving an apt reply— and how good is a timely word! (Proverbs 15:23)

A word fitly spoken is like apples of gold in pictures of silver. (Proverbs 25:11)

Let my mouth be filled with your praise and with your honor all the day. (Psalm 71:8)

Give praise to the Lord, proclaim his name; make known among the nations what he has done. (Psalm 105:1)

Some people make cutting remarks, but the words of the wise bring healing. (Proverbs 12:18)

Gracious words are like a honeycomb, sweetness to the soul and health to the body. (Proverbs 16:24)

✦ Powerful speech is better than fancy speech.

Peter's first sermon in Jerusalem won "about three thousand souls" to God. (Acts 2:41)

And my speech and my preaching was not with enticing words of man's wisdom, but in demonstration of the Spirit and of power. (1 Corinthians 2:4)

✦ You will enjoy life much more if your speech is wise and godly.

Words satisfy the mind as much as fruit does the stomach; good talk is as gratifying as a good harvest. (Proverbs 18:20)

A friendly discussion is as stimulating as the sparks that fly when iron strikes iron. (Proverbs 27:17, TLB)

Part 3: FEED

What does the Bible say about communicating?

✦ **The best communication is face to face.**

But we, brethren, being taken from you for a short time in presence, not in heart, endeavored the more abundantly to see your face with great desire. (1 Thessalonians 2:17)

✦ **God will give you understanding of what to say as well as how to say it.**

The Lord GOD has given me the tongue of those who are taught, that I may know how to sustain with a word him who is weary. Morning by morning he awakens; he awakens my ear to hear as those who are taught. (Isaiah 50:4, ESV)

✦ **Good people speak good words.**

A good man brings good things out of the good stored up in his heart, and an evil man brings evil things out of the evil stored up in his heart. For the mouth speaks what the heart is full of. (Luke 6:45)

✦ **Relate to people through something or someone you have in common.**

Because he was a tent maker as they were, he stayed and worked with them. (Acts 18:3)

✦ **Use wholesome language.**

Words from the mouth of the wise are gracious. (Ecclesiastes 10:12)

Don't use foul or abusive language. Let everything you say be good and helpful, so that your words will be an encouragement to those who hear them. (Ephesians 4:29, NLT)

But now you also, put them all aside: anger, wrath, malice, slander, and abusive speech from your mouth. (Colossians 3:8)

Do not repay evil with evil or insult with insult. On the contrary, repay evil with blessing, because to this you were called so that you may inherit a blessing. (1 Peter 3:9)

✦ Use pleasant, gentle words.

A gentle answer deflects anger, but harsh words make tempers flare. The tongue of the wise makes knowledge appealing, but the mouth of a fool belches out foolishness. (Proverbs 15:1-2)

Gentle words are a tree of life; a deceitful tongue crushes the spirit. (Proverbs 15:4)

Pleasant words are persuasive. (Proverbs 16:21)

But the wisdom that is from above is first pure, then peaceable, gentle, and easy to be entreated, full of mercy and good fruits, without partiality, and without hypocrisy. (James 3:17)

✦ Put your heart into your communications.

So being affectionately desirous of you, we were willing to have imparted unto you, not the gospel of God only, <u>but also our own souls</u>, because ye were dear unto us. (1 Thessalonians 2:8)

✦ Be truthful.

We will speak the truth in love, growing in every way more and more like Christ. (Ephesians 4:15)

Wounds from a sincere friend are better than many kisses from an enemy. (Proverbs 27:6)

Let a righteous man strike me—it is a kindness; let him rebuke me—it is oil for my head; let my head not refuse it. (Psalm 141:5)

But correct the wise, and they will love you. (Proverbs 9:8b)

✦ Know when to keep quiet. God gave us two ears and one mouth.

Everyone should be quick to listen, slow to speak. (James 1:19)

So don't bother correcting mockers; they will only hate you. (Proverbs 9:8a)

A gossip betrays a confidence, but a trustworthy person keeps a secret. (Proverbs 11:13)

Those who control their tongue will have a long life; opening your mouth can ruin everything. (Proverbs 13:3)

Even fools are thought wise when they keep silent; with their mouths shut, they seem intelligent. (Proverbs 17:28)

Whoever keeps his mouth and his tongue keeps himself out of trouble. (Proverbs 21:23)

◆ **Speak with right motives.**

Whatsoever you do, do all to the glory of God. (1 Corinthians 10:31)

◆ **Speak up for others.**

Speak up for those who cannot speak for themselves, for the rights of all who are destitute. (Proverbs 15:4)

Defend the poor and fatherless. (Psalm 82:3)

◆ **Listen well. Note what is being left out. Notice facial expressions and tone of voice.**

The simple believe anything, but the prudent give thought to their steps. (Proverbs 14:15)

Test all things; hold fast what is good. (1 Thessalonians 5:21)

◆ **Are you interested in understanding or do you just want to hear yourself talk?**

Fools have no interest in understanding; they only want to air their own opinions. (Proverbs 18:2)

Spouting off before listening to the facts is both shameful and foolish. (Proverbs 18:13)

◆ **Be persuasive.**

And he reasoned in the synagogue every Sabbath, and persuaded the Jews and the Greeks. (Acts 18:4)

◆ **Use word pictures. Use unforgettable stories.**

Jesus told them a story. (Luke 18:1)

Part 4: DEED

How can I communicate better?

✦ **Make someone's day with a smile and a compliment.
Most people need recognition and encouragement.**

*Heaviness in the heart of man makes it stoop: but a good word makes it glad.
(Proverbs 12:25)*

The Lord GOD has given me the tongue of the learned, that I should know how to speak a word in season to him that is weary. (Isaiah 50:4)

✦ **Don't ramble on. Be succinct and to the point.**

*Whoever guards his mouth preserves his life; he who opens wide his lips comes to ruin.
(Proverbs 13:3)*

Hard work always pays off; mere talk puts no bread on the table. (Proverbs 14:23)

The man of few words and settled mind is wise. (Proverbs 17:27)

Let your words be few. (Ecclesiastes 5:2)

But above all, my brethren, do not swear, either by heaven or by earth or with any other oath; but your yes is to be yes, and your no, no, so that you may not fall under judgment. (James 5:11)

✦ **Don't tell everything you know. Think before you speak.**

*The wise don't make a show of their knowledge, but fools broadcast their foolishness.
(Proverbs 12:23)*

*Don't shoot off your mouth, or speak before you think. Don't be too quick to tell God what you think he wants to hear. God's in charge, not you—the less you speak, the better.
(Ecclesiastes 5:2, The Message)*

✦ **Express your feelings!**

Open rebuke is better than secret love. (Proverbs 27:5)

✦ **Approach at the right time: not by demanding an audience.**

There is a time there for every purpose and for every work. (Ecclesiastes 3:17)

✦ **Don't spread rumors or gossip.**

Where no wood is, there the fire goes out: So where there is no talebearer, the strife ceases. (Proverbs 26:20)

✦ **Try to get the other person to talk. Don't dominate the conversation. Be considerate.**

In lowliness of mind let each esteem other better than themselves. (Philippians 2:3)

✦ **Listen first. Talk second.**

Rephrase what you heard to make sure you understood what the speaker meant.
Maintain eye contact as if the speaker is the only person in the whole world.
Ask the speaker questions. Be an active hearer.
Agree with the speaker's feelings. Don't judge their communications. Unity and agreement are powerful.

Sample Lesson on Interpersonal Communications

INDEX

30 Ways to Mess Up Your Class (59)

attendance (51)

authority over demons (23)

bad breath (60)

building points (30, 33, 34, 38)

blessings of being a teacher (11)

Berea (60)

Bible is Jesus! (11)

binding (restricting) the devil from your class (23)

bless the class (26)

blood of Jesus (26)

bondage to the devil (25, 76)

Caring heart. (15)

challenging questions (60)

characteristics of good stories (53, 54)

charts (57)

chronological list (57)

class participation (35, 36, 59)

closing (29) with a blessing or a prayer

common errors (59)

comparison and contrast (55)

concordance (33)

Confederacy (24)

consequences of not applying the lesson (28, 38, 39)

contrast (55)

counting the cost (16)

cut and paste (33)

DEED: Challenging your students to apply the lesson and pointing out specific ways to put their knowledge into action (30)

defeated Satan (23)

defining your topic (31)

develop others into teachers (16)

do your best in teaching (45)

drama (9)

earthly honor (12)

easy to understand (31)

encourage questions (36)

encouraging students to contribute their thoughts (35)

enemies of integrity (18)

eternal honor (11)

everyday language (54)

fatigue (18)

favoring certain students (60)

fear of burn-out (18)

fear of failure (18)

FEED: Leading the class through a progressive examination of your topic, point by point (30)

foundation (biblical definition of the principle (38)

gathering Bible verses (33)

getting their attention (31)

God expects more from you (13)

God's anointing (14)

God's plan for your student (21)

Good models (Dedication, 60)

graphics (57)

greet the class (27)

His face shine upon you (29)

"How" is critical to students (59)

humor (54)

illustrations (38)

insight into your students (21)

inspiration for the subject (30)

introduce yourself to the class (27)

Jesus' favorite teaching method (55)

judgment (51)

kindness and peace (11)

king and a priest unto God (23)

liar (19)

life speaks louder than your words (14)

loose God's blessings upon your class (26)

minister (9)

motivating your class (32)

mouthwash (60)

NEED: Clarifying the need for your students to learn and practice this teaching in their lives (32)

negative motivation (32)

Noah (51)

opportunities presented by a question (47)

passion for the Bible (15)

pastor's support (51)

patience (21)

Paul's Pattern for Presentations (27)

perfect practice makes perfect (45)

personal life of the teacher (17)

persuade (9)

pictures and graphics (57)

positive motivation (32)

practical application (74)

practice (45)

prayed for your class (16)

prayer and praise reports (9)

preparation checklist (45)

preparing and delivering the lesson (30)

proclaim the blessings of the Lord (26)

Index

rewards (32)

royal priest (23)

salesperson (9)

Sample Lesson: Divine Healing (126)

Sample Lesson: Freedom from Sin (75)

Sample Lesson: God's Sovereignty (121)

Sample Lesson: God's Will (65)

Sample Lesson: Heaven (133)

Sample Lesson: Interpersonal Communication (156)

Sample Lesson: Joy (117)

Sample Lesson: Money Management (141)

Sample Lesson: Prayer (91)

Sample Lesson: Taking the Name of God in Vain (151)

Sample Lesson: Teamwork (101)

Sample Lesson: Spiritual Warfare (81)

Sample Lesson: Suffering (107)

secret weapon of teachers: stories (53)

SEED: The biblical definition of your topic (30)

seeing the person your student will become (21)

sexual purity (17)

spiritual warfare (23)

stories (53)

stress (18)

submission of demons to Christians (25)

teachable moment (36)

teacher participation in class discussions (35, 36)

teaching too long (60)

Techniques to Gain Class Participation (35)

Poem: The Precious Moment (47)

Topical Lessons (30)

Useful In-Class Comments (43)

visionary leader (10)

Why People Come to Class (19)

your own true identity (23)

Bibliography

Spiritual Warfare for Every Christian by Dean Sherman with Bill Payne. Published by Youth with a Mission Publishing: 1990. P.O. Box 55787, Seattle, Washington 98155 www.YWAMPublishing.com

The Student Bible Dictionary by Karen Dockrey, Johnnie Godwin, Phyllis Godwin: Barbour Publishing, Incorporated, 2000. P.O. Box 719 Uhrichsville, Ohio 44883 www.BarbourBooks.com

Rose Book of Bible Charts, Maps, and Timelines. RW Research, Inc. 2005. Rose Publishing. 4455 Torrance Blvd., 259 Torrance, California 90503 www.Rose-Publishing.com

www.EastonsBible Dictionary.com

Dr. Paul Chappell. *When Jesus Gave Thanks* http://www.dailyintheword.org/content/when-jesus-gave-thanks%E2%80%A6

Jack Wellman, Christian Crier, *What Is the Biblical Definition of Joy? How Does the Bible Define Joy?*, May 21, 2015. Retrieved on December 17, 2016. http://www.patheos.com/blogs/christiancrier/2015/05/21/what-is-the-biblical-definition-of-joy-how-does-the-bible-define-joy/

David P. Scaer and D. Miall Edwards, *Joy.* 1997. Retrieved on December 17, 2016. http://www.BibleStudyTools.com/Dictionary/Joy

Koehler, Paul F. *Biblical Storytelling in Oral Cultures.* William Carey Library. 2010. Pasadena, CA. www.MissionBooks.org

Other books by Curtis Mosley

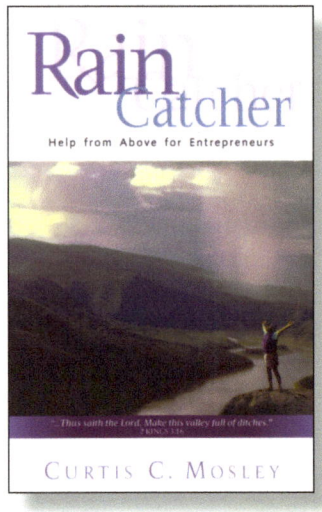

RainCatcher: Help from Above for Entrepreneurs contains the inspiration that motivated the author to start a highly successful business. It is based on the scriptural teaching that God blesses those who put themselves in a place to be blessed. Although many trainers speak about great salesmen as "rain makers," this book turns that old concept upside down, teaching us to be "rain catchers," or recipients of God's outpouring.

The most prominent Christian businessman of his day, Archie Dunham, chairman of Conoco, endorsed the book whole heartedly, as "easy to read and timely."

TeamWeaver, the Ten Greatest Teams in the Bible, is an entertaining and enlightening analysis of scripture's ten greatest teams. You may be able to guess some of the teams included in this book, such as David and his army and the first century church, but have you considered Elijah and Elisha? Mordecai and Esther? There are plenty of surprises in this new look at what ingredients make up a great team.

Pat Williams, Senior Vice President of the Orlando Magic, and the world's foremost expert on teamwork, wrote the Foreword for this book. He said that he delved into the book with new enthusiasm and described it as "original" and "fresh." Additionally, pastors often preach from TeamWeaver and Christian university professors use it to teach students how to work together in study teams.

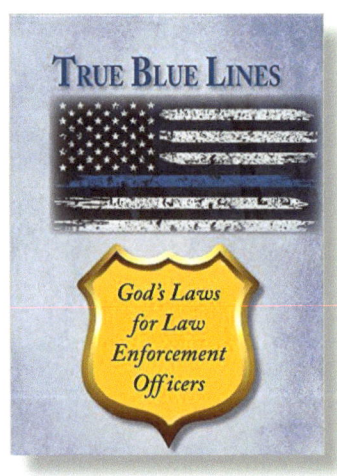

True Blue Lines, God's Laws for Law Enforcement Officers, is a Christian book for all those in law enforcement. It is a wonderful source of inspiration to those who deal with danger, stress, and the tough challenges of a hard profession. The book is organized into two parts: the first half contains Bible verses divided into 65 topics such as Ability, Emergencies, and PTSD; the second half has 36 true-life stories of heroism by law enforcement officers who faced great danger in the line of duty. These thrilling stories include daring confrontations with terrorists and other dangerous, hardened criminals. There are also over 130 photos in the book. The Scriptures and stories herein are relevant to both the professional and personal lives of peace officers. Godliness is profitable for this life and the life to come. This book will have an impact on officers now and forever. True Blue Lines fills the gap between professional technical training and personal character development. It also impresses upon our men and women in uniform that the chain of command is important, training is critical, and noble conduct is expected. There is no better source for wisdom that the Bible and this book makes it easy to find the Scripture needed for a particular situation. True Blue Lines has an influence that goes far beyond the individual officers to their families, victims of crimes, and the community at large. True Blue Lines is a work with far reaching impact.

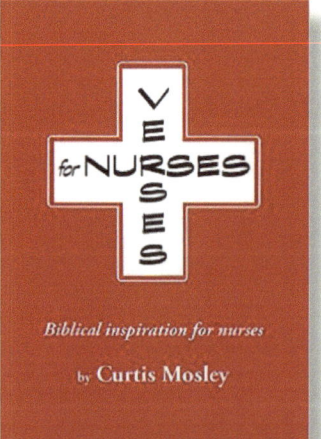

Verses for Nurses is a powerful, biblically based inspirational text for nurses and nursing students. It provides Bible verses of inspiration, encouragement, and instruction for 46 nursing topics. When faced with a demanding situation, a nurse can find the Scriptures pertinent to the current circumstance. Additionally, Verses for Nurses contains 19 true-life stories about heroic nurses in critical and emergency scenarios. This book builds character, inspires boldness, and promotes professionalism. Because it is the ideal gift for nursing school graduates, a number of Christian nursing schools have given Verses for Nurses to their seniors on Pinning Day.

www.ingramcontent.com/pod-product-compliance
Lightning Source LLC
Chambersburg PA
CBHW042146290426
44110CB00003B/133